Developing a Learning Organization

Developing a Learning Organization

Peter Lassey

KOGAN PAGE

YOURS TO HAVE AND TO HOLD

BUT NOT TO COPY

First published in 1998

Kogan Page Limited
120 Pentonville Road
London N1 9JN

British Library Cataloguing in Publication Data

A CIP record for this book is available from the British Library.

ISBN 0 7494 2413 3

Typeset by JS Typesetting, Wellingborough, Northants.
Printed in England by Clays Ltd, St Ives plc

To Moira and Alice,
from whom I learn more and more,
each day

CONTENTS

Contents

ACKNOWLEDGEMENTS

I would like to thank a number of people who have given me their views on the emerging manuscript, especially William Blacklock and my good friend and colleague Anne Macintosh for their help and guidance; the Museum Training Institute and the Management Charter Initiative for permission to reproduce units from their occupational standards and Investors in People UK and the Qualification and Curriculum Authority for permission to reproduce their standards and criteria respectively.

I would also like to thank Mike McGowan of POINT, for designing the figures and Philip Mudd of Kogan Page for his support and encouragement, and finally, my family for their continued love and support. Any errors that remain are mine alone.

PREFACE

If organizations are to gain a competitive advantage in a changing world they need to have the ability to adapt constantly to new circumstances and challenges. Yet organizations are simply collections of people who share common goals, only some of whom embrace change. Therefore, if we want an organization to adapt to take advantage of the new circumstances, then we also want whole collections of people to continually change their behaviour. Consequently, the aim of this book is to show how organizations can develop a culture where learning is encouraged.

Chapter 1 examines the rationale behind the 'Learning organization' concept and outlines how the learning organization differs from traditional organizations. The remainder of the book is broken down into three parts. Part 1 looks at the structures within the organization that can help to develop and nurture a learning organization. It examines how occupational standards of competence can be used to facilitate a coherent set of systems and procedures, job descriptions and appraisal systems, which will provide the foundation of the learning organization.

Part 2 looks at developing people within the organization. It examines how people can develop solutions to business problems and how flexible training and development activities can be implemented to meet learning needs.

Part 3 looks at how the different initiatives in Parts 1 and 2 can help to provide external recognition for the organization and its people through NVQ, IiP and ISO 9000 certification. The book aims to pull together a number of different initiatives and show how they can be integrated to provide the basis of developing a learning organization.

For the sake of simplicity I have used the pronoun 'she' and 'her' throughout this book as shorthand for 'he or she' and 'him and her'. Hopefully, there will be a time in the future when referring to individuals in management or authority positions in the feminine, will not seem as strange as it sometimes does, even today.

If you have any comments, good or bad on any part of this book I would be grateful for the opportunity to learn from them. Please feel free to write to me, c/o Philip Mudd, at Kogan Page Limited, 120 Pentonville Road, London, N1 9JN.

Peter Lassey

1

DEVELOPING A LEARNING ORGANIZATION

INTRODUCTION

We are living in a changing world where each generation has to adapt to greater and greater change in an ever shortening timespan. Technological change is having an enormous impact on all our lives. Today, society is far more sophisticated than the world into which we were born. As leaps in technology become greater and greater, our ability to predict future developments with any certainty becomes more and more problematic, creating a difficulty in planning for future change.

As individuals, if we wish for success in this changing world we keep pace with world events, technological developments and the development of ideas. We constantly analyse this information and change our activities and ideas in response to the changing world. Yes, we learn. Successful people have the ability to, and are prepared to change and adapt. Successful people are people who learn. Organizations are no different, successful organizations are *learning organizations*.

There is a saying, 'If you always do what you always did, you will always get what you have always got.' Without learning there is no improvement and without improvement organizations stagnate. In reality, all organizations do learn. All organizations train their staff. All organizations develop new concepts and methods of working to cope with changing situations. However, *too many* organizations learn painfully slowly; they train their staff badly and develop to new situations long after the most successful organizations.

For most managers, change should be avoided wherever possible. Often they feel that change will destroy morale and lead to uncertainty and a lack of stability. Of course, this is the view of many organizations but not the view of the most successful organizations. Successful organizations embrace change and development as the most important factor in the success of the organization. Learning organizations have the capacity to reconstruct themselves rather than be dependent upon external pressures, learning organizations are able to exert a level of control on their environment rather than be slaves to it.

A learning organization:

- understands that its future is dependent upon the abilities of all its people
- provides opportunities for the personal development of those people
- recognizes that people learn in different ways
- encourages all its people to learn, innovate and contribute to its future.

The prize that awaits a learning organization is simple: success. As a learning organization, staff turnover will slow down, the organization will become more attractive to potential employees therefore enabling better quality recruitment. The organization will be able to respond to new events and situations quicker than rivals, able to exploit its advantage. The ability of the organization to focus on organizational goals and secure staff commitment to their achievement will lead to far greater efficiency and a better quality of product or service.

Learning organizations rely on individual learners, who, in order to learn need to:

- recognize that they can learn
- identify the learning outcomes
- identify and utilize the support available.

WE ALL CAN LEARN

A generally accepted definition of learning is the changing of behaviour, not simply on a theoretical level but on the level of everyday experience. We talk about learning to walk, drive, accept criticism and live with someone else. Indeed, as all parents quickly realize, all human beings are created not only with an ability but an almost obsessive compulsion to learn. Yet, the structures that we use as a society to assist each other to learn, tend to cater for a specific type of learner, consequently labelling others as unable to learn at an early stage. Evidently, this is not the case, and yet the priorities of the education system and society's attitude to a particular form of *academic learning,* as opposed to any other type, lead to the whole issue of learning being value laden. It is easy to form the impression that learning equates exclusively with increasing knowledge, and education with bestowing that body of knowledge.

In one sense, it is a self-fulfilling prophecy. Society values the acquisition of knowledge and insight above all else. Society is governed by people who have been successful at that acquisition of knowledge and they in turn encourage the valuing of such *academic* learning. However, it would be foolish to underestimate the immense value of knowledge and understanding in the learning process. At the same time, the acquisition of knowledge is *just one part of the learning experience.* Alongside knowledge, an individual needs opportunities to practise the new behaviour, and a willingness and confidence to attempt the new behaviour, as well as a whole raft of other skills and abilities such as common sense, interpersonal skills and self-knowledge to name but a few.

Learning is an active and cooperative process and depends on the willingness of those concerned. There is an old saying, 'You cannot teach an old dog new tricks,' well you can, but only if the old dog wants to learn. For an individual to become a learner it requires the commitment of that individual, for an organization to become a learning organization it requires the commitment from all staff. A learning organization is not one whereby all the individuals in the organization learn but where the organization collectively learns.

Collective learning

What do we mean by collective learning? Well, this is where a change in the behaviour of one individual leads to appropriate responses, perhaps learning responses, from others in the organization. It is where a change in behaviour of one individual has an effect on others in the organization. For this to happen people need to be committed to helping each other achieve their learning goals, not simply to be committed to their own. People need to be involved in, and to understand the learning activities of their colleagues.

Surprisingly, many quite senior managers of organizations still view the development of staff and especially the acquisition of qualifications as a threat. Often, there is an assumption that providing training and development or qualifications will mean investing in an individual who will eventually leave, as if this was something that should never happen. Healthy organizations recognize that a degree of staff turnover is not only a fact of life but necessary to a dynamic, robust and adaptable organization. A learning organization depends on a continuing contribution from its staff to prosper. If the staff, for whatever reason, decide that they no longer wish to contribute to the development of the organization it is important that they are able to leave. New willing staff can be recruited to make that contribution. If it is felt that this turnover is excessive then it should be addressed just as any other problem encountered by the organization. People leave organizations for many reasons, but people do not usually leave simply because they can.

Fostering a culture where learning and assisting each other to achieve and develop themselves will have many benefits, including:

- increased motivation *leading* to increased productivity
- a competent work-force *leading* to fewer mistakes
- improved working practices *leading* to lower operating costs
- a happier work-force *leading* to lower staff turnover.

Often the first step towards development is to demonstrate to learners that they had to learn the skills they already possess. As they realize what they have achieved, they can be shown that the acquisition of new skills can be just as painless.

Vast numbers of people spend hours discussing the finer points of character development, structure and the social, political and economic subtexts of extremely complex narratives. If these texts were historical novels and the discussion was articulated in the accepted academic mode of discourse, it would be seen as a very worthy academic discipline. However, since the discussion is about television soap operas and articulated in a different way, it is frowned upon. Many of us can discuss the finer points of aesthetics, strategy and philosophy at a very complex and learned level. Yet because it is in relation to association football it is outside the educational establishment, and it is the educational establishment that bestows value on that which is learned. Maybe it comes down to the fact that some people are lucky to be interested in physics, mathematics, history, etc. They have an interest in areas that are part of the academic curriculum and are catered for. Others have interests in different areas that fall outside and are accordingly disadvantaged as their interests are not catered for. No matter how reductionist and simplistic this argument is, it does serve to show that an educational system which is built on homage to the values and thought of a previous age, serves to restrict our understanding of learning to a rather narrow band of experience.

How we learn

Learning is our most important attribute, but just as everyone has different characteristics and traits they also have different learning abilities and as such, respond to different stimuli. For most of us, the way we usually learn is to search out information and advice relating to the subject that interests us. Often this is a TV programme, a book, a friend or family member. Only rarely would we look to the educational establishment for the learning and then mainly when we need recognition for that learning. The same is true for how we learn at work. Mostly, we find out how to operate new machinery or how to achieve new tasks by asking and observing other colleagues. Eventually we become proficient after much trial and error, usually lots of error. However, because we learn out of necessity rather than as part of a plan, we are always 'fire-fighting,' learning through crisis situations.

Learning from colleagues is a very efficient and cost effective method for learning. It means that only essential skills are passed on. Since the employees are still working, there is very little time-off for the employee, and therefore very little cost to the employer.

To demonstrate to an individual that they have this capacity to learn, simply ask them to think back to soon after they started in their current job and ask them about what activities or tasks caused them problems. Then simply ask them how did they learn to do that task better? Did a colleague help them? Did they read a manual? Did they watch others?

A learning organization does not stop this form of learning, it merely harnesses it in order to maximize the potential of its work-force. Learning organizations train their personnel to be aware of training and development opportunities for themselves and others. They train managers to help identify development goals with their staff and help their staff to reach those goals.

IDENTIFYING THE LEARNING OUTCOMES

Successful people and successful organizations don't just learn, they plan their learning. The real skill is not to learn skills which you should already have, but to develop skills which you will need in the future, in short, to be a proactive learner. To do this effectively, the manager needs to accurately assess the skills their staff already possess, identify the skills they are likely to need in the short and longer term, and plan a personal development path which will provide those skills. Skill is probably the wrong word to use as it has rather a narrow usage in terms of personal development. A more accurate term would be one which has wide acceptance in the training and development sector already: *competence.*

Competence infers far more than simply 'skills'. For someone to be competent, they would need to be able to apply all the relevant skills and knowledge, in the right measure and at the right time, in a real work situation. This should surely be our aim, this is what all employers would wish of their staff. Our challenge then, is not to develop skills, but to develop competence.

Describing competence

Describing and defining occupational competence is time consuming and resource intensive, but luckily, most employers have had this done for them with the production of national occupational standards by Industry Lead Bodies (ILBs). Many of these ILBs have been superseded by National Training Organizations who will take on the responsibility of reviewing and revising these standards.

These standards are an attempt by representatives of different industries or sectors to define what competence means for their industry. Copies of these standards can be obtained from a number of sources and can provide a very useful starting point for identifying current and future competence needs. Standards can be obtained from the Qualifications and Curriculum Authority (QCA) database, but usually more user-friendly versions are available from the ILB that produced the standards. The QCA will direct you to the relevant Lead Body if you are in any doubt.

If the learning needs of an individual are to assist them to perform competently in their current job, or to prepare them to perform competently in a future job role, the starting point should be the description of each job role in terms of what constitutes competent performance. This calls for a systematic approach from the organization in defining the roles and responsibilities of each job role and what constitutes competent performance for each job role. This can be achieved in a number of ways and can be described by a plethora of different documents such as job descriptions, personnel specifications, job specifications, standard procedures, to name but a few.

It is important to provide clear descriptions of what is deemed competent performance for each job role. There is always a danger that the large array of different documents can lead to numerous descriptions of performance, all of which are slightly different; not a recipe for clarity. By using a standard component to describe competence across all these documents we can provide greater clarity and guard against differing standards of performance. Moreover, by utilizing national occupational standards of competence, organizations can benefit from the work and investment already spent on identifying and describing performance.

IDENTIFYING AND UTILIZING SUPPORT

Understanding that your organization needs to be a learning organization and realizing that goal, is not necessarily straightforward. As mentioned previously, successful organizations harness the informal learning networks, and utilize the existing competence of staff to maximize the development potential of the organization.

The learning organization needs not simply to provide a structure which will allow learning to take place, they also need to encourage and support learning. Encouragement can be done through the organization's reward system (pay, promotion, etc), through the monitoring and appraisal system, but most effectively through the organization's culture (its beliefs and attitudes).

The learning organization needs to ensure that the learning process makes the learner conscious of the process, becoming a participant in the process rather than a recipient. The learner needs to be able to:

- assess current performance
- set down goals
- collect and analyse (objectively) data about their performance
- be open and honest with colleagues
- relate to colleagues as a potential resource for learning.

Other colleagues can act as mentors or guides for the learner. Their role would be to:

- convey respect and support
- provide accurate feedback in a positive manner
- listen empathetically
- encourage thinking by asking probing questions.

The ability of an individual to learn from their experiences is dependent upon the individual's ability to learn how to learn. However, the learner's ability to learn is only one factor in determining the learning of an individual. Other factors will include the organization's structures, such as job descriptions, performance appraisals etc, the opportunities made available for learning and the learning culture.

Some simple changes to the way the organization operates can make a huge difference to the culture and environment of the organization. This will in itself make an enormous leap towards the organization becoming a learning organization.

THE LEARNING ORGANIZATION

The definition of a learning organization is somewhat elusive. Many have proffered a definition, Malthotra defines a learning organization as an 'organization with an ingrained philosophy for anticipating, reacting and responding to change, complexity and uncertainty' (Malhotra, 1996). Most definitions are valid to some degree but possibly the closest to the essence is from Joop Swieringa and André Wierdsma who explain 'learning organizations are not only capable of learning, but also of *learning to learn*. In other words, they are not only able to *become* competent but also to *remain* competent' (Swieringa and Wierdsma, 1992).

The key to understanding the learning organization is *development*. If learning is about the changing of behaviour then a learning organization is capable of changing its behaviour. A learning organization can adapt, transform and develop itself. In other words, it is an organization that can respond to new challenges and changes in the wider environment.

However, a learning organization is not simply one where all the individuals are active learners. Organizational learning is built upon the abilities of individuals to learn but it is much more than the sum of the learning of those individuals. Argyris and Schön as long ago as 1978 pointed out that 'there is no organizational learning without individual learning, and that individual learning is necessary but insufficient condition for organizational learning'. Swieringa and Wierdsma (1992) take it one step further to explain that only when 'the change in the behaviour of one individual has an effect on the behaviour of others' can it be said that the organization is becoming a learning organization.

Organizational learning is a *collective* activity, actions must be understood by others in the organization so that appropriate learning responses can be made. Others within the organization need time to acquire a collective competence and assist each other in learning.

It can be argued that organizations only exist in the minds of its members in the sense that without cooperation between the individuals that make up the organization, it cannot function. The organization itself only manifests itself in the behaviour of its people. So, if an organization learns, there is a mutual changing of behaviour, therefore *organizational learning is equivalent to organizational change.*

All learning organizations are different. It would be a brave person indeed who would tempt fate to say that their organization is a learning organization. It would probably be more useful to say that the learning organization is a goal that all organizations can aspire to. Although it is possible to identify the many different constituents which contribute towards that goal it is not possible to prescribe the route for every organization, because the people that make up the organization need to be involved in planning their route to their shared goal.

However, it is possible to examine what a learning organization looks like and explore their characteristics in order to help plan an organization's specific route. The following lists are not exhaustive but should provide a clearer view of what a learning organization looks like.

Features of organizations

Traditional organization
- punishes mistakes
- operates traditional working practices
- sends employees on training courses
- plays safe
- managers monitor and supervise staff
- discourages experimentation
- command and control management
- reviews instigated after disasters
- discourages staff suggestions

- decision based on management 'hunches'
- work is within departmental boundaries
- discourages questioning from work-force.

Learning organization
- learns from mistakes
- adapts working practices
- trains employees
- takes risks
- managers coach and develop staff
- encourages experimentation
- devolution of power
- routine reviews of activities
- encourages staff suggestions
- decisions based on empirical data
- work is across departmental boundaries
- encourages questioning from work-force.

Attitudes which underpin organizations

Traditional organization
- learning develops the individual
- management is the source of new ideas
- learning is for beginners
- staff viewed as cost
- learners as recipients
- no trust
- individual memory.

Learning organization
- learning develops the organization
- work-force is the source of new ideas
- learning is for everyone
- staff viewed as resource
- learners as co-creative
- trust
- organizational memory.

Learning levels

Organizations have rules which prescribe the behaviour required of individuals. When individual learning occurs, the individual refines and perfects their behaviour in order to better achieve the results they wish to attain. An individual will learn by analysing her behaviour in relation to the results achieved and noticing how variations in her behaviour can affect the results consequently changing her behaviour to affect the results. (This learning may not be of benefit to the organization in terms of increased productivity or workmanship, it may simply be of benefit to the individual.) For example, greater productivity may mean that the individual could finish work earlier, or simply it makes the job easier. As long as the rules lead to behaviour which achieves the required results then, individual learning is all that is required.

Organizational learning or collective learning begins when there is a recognition that the rules no longer lead to behaviour that produces the correct results and the collective behaviour and the rules that govern that behaviour are changed at the same time (see Figure 1.1).

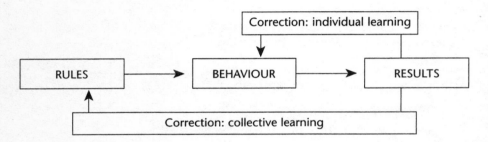

Figure 1.1 Organizational or collective learning
Source: Swieringa and Wierdsma (1992)

This level of learning is called single loop learning and is the basic level of collective or organizational learning, Swieringa and Wierdsma have taken Argyris and Schön's work on single and double loop learning and expanded it to take account of a further level of learning that they describe as triple loop learning.

The different learning levels are defined in terms of the relationship between the perceived problem and the scope for its resolution, through a hierarchy of possible interventions.

● Single loop learning is where the collective learning causes changes in the rules that govern action for the organization. These rules may be implicit or explicit. At this level of learning the effectiveness of the rules is questioned and the rules are adapted.

A small fast food outlet on a busy high street has seen its profits fall significantly over time. The management decide to place advertisements in the local press, expand the menu and provide inducements for regulars.

- Double loop learning is where the collective learning causes changes to the insights which determine the rules. At this level of learning the rules themselves are questioned in terms of why they are there and why they deliver the type of behaviour that is needed.

  The management decide to examine the name of the outlet, the range of food it offers, and its location in a bid to stop the customer base from dwindling.

- Triple loop learning is where the collective learning causes changes in the principles upon which the organization was founded. At this level of learning, the role or the mission of the organization is questioned.

  The management conclude that there is no longer a market for a business such as theirs in that location. It is decided to change the nature of the business to reflect the changing nature of the area. After a short closure for a refit the business reopens as a café, with a new name. The new organization could specialize in a small selection of higher priced items in a pleasant atmosphere. The management identified that the customer base was changing and in order to survive as a business it needed to attract a completely different clientele.

Many organizations may question the rules, the insights or principles upon which they operate, that in itself is not the mark of a learning organization. The levels of learning are successive from single to double to triple. The successful learning organization is multilateral, it moves through the different levels, with the progression from one to another based upon collective learning. Or in other words, the real skill is not in operating at any particular level, it is in knowing which level is appropriate for the situation in which the organization finds itself. In the example above, the fast food outlet continued to lose money every day that the problem was not addressed. The progression through the different stages shows that the organization learns, however the effectiveness of the organization as a learning organization is not so much about reaching the solution as it is about the speed at which it reaches that solution. If an organization learns too slowly, it could flounder long before it reaches the solution.

Communication

Crucial to the ability of an organization to learn is a healthy communication system, and one which encourages questioning of the organization's activities and one which values and encourages the input of employees at all levels. Organizations may be compared to one of the most incredibly complex yet effective learning systems, namely ourselves. The decision-making abilities of the organism rely on prompt responses from the nervous system to determine its activity or movement. Just as our nervous system responds almost instantaneously to warn of any potential threat, each organization should have a responsive and effective communication system which will provide accurate feedback so that informed decisions can be made to change the activities of the organization, and so thereby enabling it to perform more effectively and avoid danger. To an organization, an effective communication system is its senses and its central nervous system. Without one, it does not have the information to make valid decisions.

The strategy

If the development of a learning organization is the goal, what is the strategy? The road to a learning organization is a slow and never ending journey. Slow, in that it is a process of evolution rather than revolution. One where the strengths of the organization are built upon and the weaknesses are gradually eliminated; a journey on which the whole organization must travel. Never ending in that just as learning is a continual process, becoming a learning organization is a continual process. A learning organization is constantly adapting and changing to accommodate changing times. However, every journey begins with one step and the first step for this journey is to realize the organizational imperative to become a learning organization. For many, this does not require a leap of faith for as Senge (1990) reminds us 'The rate at which organizations learn may become the only sustainable source of competitive advantage', quoted by Malhotra (1996).

Once the organizational imperative has been realized, this vision needs to be shared with all employees. Without their commitment to this vision it cannot succeed. Indeed, the nature of the learning organization itself will be dependant upon their input. A shared vision and a commitment to a learning organization is only the beginning.

A change in the role of management is important to the development of a learning organization. The manager's role is to move from one of monitoring and supervising of staff to one of coaching and developing staff. It is important that managers are committed to their role change and are supported and equipped to make that change. The manager can help to build the shared vision of the learning organization and help to expand the capabilities and the aspirations of their staff and promote a learning culture.

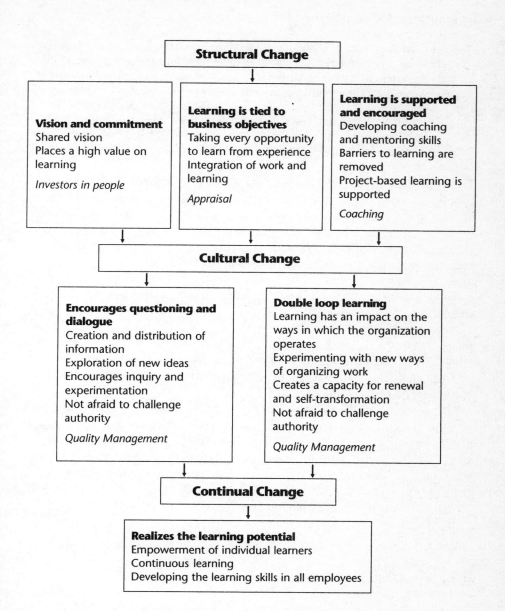

Figure 1.2 The learning organization

The management of learning

As Malhotra (1996) explains:

> A key ingredient of the Learning Organization is in *how* organizations process their managerial experiences. Learning Organizations/Managers *learn* from their experiences rather than being *bound* by their past experiences. In Generative Learning Organizations, the ability of an organization/manager is not measured by *what* it knows (that is the product of learning), but rather by *how* it learns – the process of learning. Management practices encourage, recognize, and reward: openness, systemic thinking, creativity, a sense of efficacy, and empathy.

The commitment and will to become a learning organization, important as it is, cannot transform a traditional organization unless the structures, system and practices are changed to sustain learning. As Argyris (1977) explains: 'The individuals' learning activities, in turn, are facilitated or inhibited by an ecological system of factors that may be called an organizational learning system'. The features of the organization's environment and culture will be critical in determining whether or not its 'organizational learning system' is one which encourages and supports a learning organization.

It should be remembered that a learning organization is not an easy place in which to work. Learning, changing, and re-learning is often a very difficult and even painful experience. Indeed, the calm and security of the prescriptive or bureaucratic organization is for many a far more attractive place to work.

There are a number of structural changes which will encourage and support the cultural change which will in turn help to release the potential of the learning organization. The following chapters will address these structural changes, which once made, can provide a framework from which a learning organization can evolve. This knowledge, along with a sincere will and desire to help each other achieve the common goals of the organization should provide the wherewithal to fulfil the learning potential of any organization.

PART 1: ORGANIZING THE LEARNING ENVIRONMENT

Part 1 examines how organizations can create the right environment to encourage a learning culture. It looks at the structural changes that can help to establish a healthy learning system within the organization, and how national occupational standards can be harnessed to structure the learning environment:

- how they can be tailored to meet the requirements of the organization
- how they can be used to focus the learning and development of staff around the performance critical activities
- how they can provide a benchmark across the organization's selection, recruitment, appraisal and operational systems.

2

COMPETENCE

Summary

In this chapter you will learn about:

- the concept of competence and its value
- the way that measurement of competence can help organizations to evaluate the quality of their performance
- how to develop organization-specific competence standards through tailoring existing occupational standards to meet the needs of the organization

Chapter 1 examined how the development of learners is dependent upon the identification of the learning outcomes. If the objective of a development activity is to ensure that the learner is able to perform differently, we need a measure of that performance. This will provide a mechanism for identifying any development need and also a goal for the development activity. An accurate measure of expected performance will enable the organization to target its resources and ensure that they do not expend resources developing individuals who already meet that level of performance. Moreover, such a measure of performance will allow the organization to evaluate the effectiveness of any particular training and development activity, thereby enabling the organization to learn which methods are likely to be more effective than others. Understanding the concept of competence, its value and uses underpins the development of a learning organization. Statements of competence are an effective tool for the development of individual staff, enabling learning organizations to provide a structure which will assist in the planning, delivery and evaluation of all human resource development (HRD) activities.

WHAT DO WE MEAN BY BEING COMPETENT?

When we learn, we change our behaviour, but to what end? The goal of all learning is to improve the quality of the learner's actions, or in other words, to develop behaviour which is more effective in achieving the learner's aims. What we are looking for is competence. What and how much someone learns is evident in their behaviour, therefore the measure of the improvement in that behaviour (the increase in competence) becomes a measure of the effectiveness of the learning process.

The idea of competence is well established and has various definitions; the dictionary describes someone who is competent as being adequately qualified, but this begs the question of what we mean by qualified? Essentially, being competent means to possess all the skills, knowledge, ability and confidence to perform to a generally accepted standard. Yet the term itself is meaningless unless it precedes a task, profession or occupation, since people can only be competent in relation to something, often their job.

When we think of others as competent, we think of them as safe, able and trustworthy, in short, people whom we can rely on to work without supervision. The competent person not only performs to the accepted standard but they do it consistently; they react to new and changing situations and still perform. They manage their own time and act responsibly within their job role. For employers, we are describing ideal employees. For individuals we are describing the colleagues of theirs who are widely respected, the colleagues to whom people turn when problems arise.

It is important to remember at this point that we are not looking to produce robots, standard employees with standard responses to situations. Not only is this an unrealistic goal but it actually acts against the creation of a dynamic learning organization. Innovative solutions to new problems or situations are found by the creative and enthusiastic teamwork of individuals from different backgrounds and histories, people who may address problems from different angles. What is really revolutionary about developing competence is that we look to develop people's abilities to operate without specifying a particular way of achieving the necessary outcomes. The flexibility for the individual to change the established way of operating is built into the actual concept of competence.

What constitutes competence?

If job competence is to be our development goal, the first step is to define what we mean by competence for a particular job. Some elements of competence are relatively easy to define, the key tasks and task related skills. However, it is easy to see how a competence model based on these factors alone would not describe the competent individual. The competent (safe, able, trustworthy, respectable) job-holder can do much more than simply possess the skills to perform the standard tasks required of the job. Why? Because they can do it and still answer the phone, respond to requests from customers, supervise the intern, in short, they can do it in a real (and changing) work environment. The work environment often means that the job-holder may have some degree of autonomy over the allocation of priorities to tasks and is responsible for contingency management. Surely, our competent job-holder is someone who can successfully manage a number of duties at once and deal with any reasonable problem that may arise. Mansfield and Mathews (1985) see competence comprising four key elements; task skills, contingency management skills, task management skills, role/job environment skills. Thus, if we are to develop a workable model of job competence it should include:

- all the skills required for the individual to function within the job
- the knowledge to adapt to new and changing situations
- interpersonal, social and communication skills
- an understanding of the job, the organization and the industry
- basic numeracy and literacy
- a positive attitude to the success of themselves and the organization
- the confidence and a will to act.

If we are looking to develop an individual to a level where they are competent, we must create from the above points, a measurable set of criteria. This will enable us to assess the individual's current state of development and allow us to judge when the individual has achieved the required level of competence. For if we are to determine how much people have learned we must look at what they do and assess it against an accepted standard of behaviour.

In order for the standard of competence to be useful in staff development terms, it needs to be measurable and this is the big challenge. Luckily for us, the development of national occupational standards has meant that many of the issues around the structure of the criteria have already been addressed. Occupational standards are now available for the majority of occupational areas in the UK and have been produced by practitioners with a broad model of competence in mind. Although the quality of occupational standards is variable, they do provide an excellent starting point. However, in common with most 'standards', they do have drawbacks. They are designed to be used by every type of organization and 'occupational role' rather than specific jobs. Consequently, they are generic in nature, making them difficult to read, understand and interpret into particular jobs.

OCCUPATIONAL STANDARDS

All but a few sectors of industry have developed occupational standards. As an enormous amount of time, skill and finances have been directed towards producing them, it would be short-sighted if we were to ignore them. Occupational standards are descriptions of competent performance. Their structure has been developed so that they can be used to assess performance and this is where we shall start.

Each function of an occupation has been disaggregated into parts which can be assessed. These parts are called units and each of these units is made up of a number of elements. The element is what we are going to concentrate on as they form the building blocks of the competence system with units being a collection of elements and National Vocational Qualifications (NVQs) and Scottish Vocational Qualifications (SVQs) being a collection of specific units. The guidance from QCA regarding the format of standards continues to change to provide for a more 'flexible' approach to their design. This could mean that items such as 'units' and 'elements' may become redundant in the longer term.

The basis of all the descriptions of competence are the same. They should all contain an active verb, an object and conditions. Titles of units, elements and even performance criteria should conform to the following structure (although the order is not mandatory):

Active verb	Object	Conditions
Identify	an item	to determine its features and significance
Develop	teams and individuals	to enhance performance

The detail of the element describes the outcomes that a competent person should achieve in order to be deemed to have achieved the element. It will specify all the outcomes of competent performance, all the different situations and conditions under which the outcomes should be achieved and it will specify the knowledge that is critical to that performance. The three constituent parts of the element are:

- The *performance criteria* which describes all the outcomes one would expect to see from the a competent individual performing the function described in the element.
- The *range statement* which describes all the different situations and conditions under which one would expect a competent person to be able to perform. (The Management Charter Initiative have taken advantage of an increasingly flexible attitude from QCA to devise occupational standards without range statements. However, the crucial content from the range section still appears in a detailed section on

evidence requirements. It would be surprising if other standards-setting organizations do not follow their lead.)

● The *underpinning knowledge* which describes the key areas of knowledge that a competent individual should retain, especially areas which may not be obvious from competent performance.

If we think of the UK driving test as a measure of competence it is easy to see how the different parts of the test could be described as an occupational standard. In the driving test, the performance criteria are all the things that the candidate must perform for the examiner on the actual test such as the turn in the road, the emergency stop and reversing around a corner. The range statement does not correspond exactly in the driving test but it is easy to see how it could. It would probably include adverse weather conditions such as fog, rain and snow. The underpinning knowledge is clearly the highway code. If we were to express the driving test as an element of competence it may look something like Figure 2.1.

ADAPTING OCCUPATIONAL STANDARDS

It is important to remember that occupational standards have been defined by practitioners in all types of organizations in all sectors. They represent the combined wisdom of very experienced and competent individuals and they specify the national standard of competence across an array of areas. If each sector was occupied by only one organization the standards would be easy to interpret, but because they attempt to describe a standard that can be achieved by large and small, public and private sector organizations, they inevitably avoid words which are seen as problematic to particular types of organization, often at the expense of clarity. For example, in the museum, gallery and heritage sector, a number of words are used to describe the constituent parts of the organization's collection. Museums use terms such as objects, artefacts, specimens whereas heritage organizations use terms such as site, monument, house and building and art galleries use words such as paintings, installations and works of art. None of these words adequately describe or could be interpreted to mean the same as all the others. They all contain connotations which could cause confusion and misunderstandings. The solution was to use a word which is not used by any of the organizations but a word which could be interpreted by all, the word being 'item'. This makes the standards to some degree, more difficult to read and interpret for all organizations but does not mitigate against an interpretation from any of them.

For most standards the generic nature has meant that the standards are good but not very user friendly. However, that is not to say that we can not use these standards, we simply need to be aware of their structure

---

PERFORMANCE CRITERIA

(a) You can read number plates at a distance of more than 20.5 metres.
(b) You always check your driving position, mirrors and instruments before starting.
(c) You can use all the main controls smoothly, correctly, safely and at the right time.
(d) You can use mirrors and indicators at the right time.
(e) You can execute an emergency stop under control, as quickly as possible and without locking the wheels.
(f) You can reverse around a corner under full control, keeping reasonably close to the kerb without mounting or striking it.
(g) You can reverse into a parallel parking space safely and steadily.
(h) You can turn in the road without touching the kerb.
(i) You can perform all manoeuvres without causing a danger to other road users.
(j) You obey the traffic signs and road markings at all times.
(k) Your driving speed is appropriate to road and weather conditions at all times.

RANGE STATEMENTS

(i) *Main controls:* accelerator, clutch, footbrake, handbrake, steering, gears.
(ii) *Weather conditions:* fog, rain, snow, wind.

UNDERPINNING KNOWLEDGE

1. You understand the functions of the main controls.
2. You understand the meaning of all traffic signals and road markings.
3. You know and understand *The Highway Code*.

Figure 2.1 Element: driving a motor vehicle safely on the public highway

and how they need to be interpreted by the user in relation to the organization in which they are being used.

Occupational standards are a national framework from which individual interpretations can be made without effecting the standard. Any set of criteria which are open to interpretation are also open to misinterpretation either deliberately or accidentally. However, it is possible to interpret standards for groups of people without damaging the spirit or character of the standard. As an example Figure 2.2 will show how one element from the Museum Training Institute standards could be safely adapted.

We take as an example a fictitious company called Blackbird Productions, who wish to use these standards. They are a public relations organization and wish to use this standard with their conference management section. The projects that these individuals deal with, on a day-to-day basis, are conferences. The company could make a number of changes which are insignificant in terms of changes to the standards

Competence

PERFORMANCE CRITERIA	RANGE STATEMENTS
(a) The aims and objectives of the project are clearly specified and presented to all relevant people.	(i) *Appropriate documents:* project specifications, tender invitations.
(b) The significance and value of the project to the organization is clearly identified.	(ii) *People:* external organizations, sole traders, internal staff, volunteers.
(c) The relationship between the project and the organization's policies and current activities are clearly identified.	
(d) Potential uses for the project results are clearly identified.	

UNDERPINNING KNOWLEDGE

1. Organizational context
2. Legislation, regulations, codes of conduct and professional ethics.
3. Project planning, funding and management.
4. Design briefs for specialists.

(e) The tasks and other requirements of the project are clearly specified.
(f) The timescale and deadline for the project are clearly specified.
(g) The contribution of all parties to achieving the project goals is specified and agreed.
(h) Selection criteria are developed that enable people to be evaluated on their ability to meet project requirements.
(i) Progress reporting procedures and evaluation criteria are specified.
(j) Information on the project is presented in the appropriate manner.

Figure 2.2 Element: specify project aims and objectives for people

themselves but very significant in terms of making the standards understandable and comprehensible to the individual user.

There are four main areas which can be addressed without affecting the content of the standard.

1. When substituting one word for another, the substituted word or words must be subordinate expressions of the generic word being replaced.
2. The content of the performance criteria is the critical constituent – not the way it is phrased. If the performance criteria can be rewritten so that they are easier to understand this can (and should) be done.
3. The standard is a minimum so the organization may ask the employee to do more than the national standard, thereby adding procedures or actions that are organization specific.
4. The evidence requirements may specify areas of range that require performance evidence; often providing some choices for the individual, these choices can be reduced or made for the employee.

However, a few words of warning. First, the standards are designed to be flexible, so the adapting of the standards will reduce their flexibility. Second, the object of the sentence is often further defined by a range statement. Consequently, the object of the sentence should only be replaced so long as the range statements are still applicable. Even where they are still applicable, the range statement will usually need changing to coincide with the replacement. Finally, there should be a good and logical reason for the replacement of any words within the standard. Figure 2.3 shows how Figure 2.2 has been adapted for Blackbird Productions.

PERFORMANCE EVIDENCE

(a) The aims and objectives of the **conference** are clearly specified and presented to **conference proposal committee for approval prior to presentation to the client**.

(b) The significance and value of the project to **Blackbird Productions and the client** is clearly identified.

(c) The relationship between the **conference** and the **client's** policies and current activities are clearly identified.

(d) Potential uses for the **conference outcomes** are clearly identified.

(e) The **key** tasks and other requirements of the **conference** are clearly specified.

(f) The timescale and deadline for the conference are clearly specified.

(g) The contribution of **Blackbird Productions, the client and contractors** to achieving the project goals is specified and agreed **with the conference proposal committee and the client**.

(h) Selection criteria are developed that enable **contractors** to be evaluated on their ability to meet **conference** requirements.

(i) **Blackbird Productions** progress reporting procedures and evaluation criteria are specified.

(j) Information on the **conference** is presented in the appropriate manner.

RANGE STATEMENTS

(i) *Appropriate documents:* **conference proposal report, contractor's** tender invitations.

(ii) **Clients and contractors:** external organizations, sole traders, volunteers.

UNDERPINNING KNOWLEDGE

1. Organizational context.
2. Legislation, regulations, codes of conduct and professional ethics.
3. Project planning, funding and management.
4. Design briefs for specialists.

Figure 2.3 Element: specify conference aims and objectives for clients and conference proposal committee

This means that part of the interpretation has already been done for the employee by their employer. These changes have simply substituted more specific words for generic ones. *The standard does not change if the change is to the object of the sentence, where the word substituted is a subordinate class of the (generic) object.* They have also added some organization-specific procedures. These changes make the interpretation of the standard more restrictive but at the same time, far more readable and understandable for the user. It may be worth making such changes and producing revised candidate materials if there are enough candidates in the organization to justify it. (It should be remembered that some awarding bodies produce excellent materials for candidates, when producing a revised version of the standards think how the revisions will work with the awarding body materials.) At this level the interpretation process is quite safe but it is always important to remember that if the standards are to be assessed as part of an accredited National or Scottish Vocational Qualification it is important that the changes are *agreed* with the awarding body. Usually this is done through consultation with the external verifier.

DESIGNING COMPETENCE STANDARDS FOR EMPLOYEES

The process of defining, using, evaluating and redefining competence standards for an organization is a familiar implementation loop process. Although each step may be quite discrete, the validity of the competencies depends on the use of the evaluation of each stage, a willingness to revisit previous stages in the process in order to improve the competencies and their application is crucial to the effective implementation of the standards of competence identified. Figure 2.4 shows an outline of the steps required to implement a competence-based approach to an organization.

To develop a set of specific competence standards for an individual we need to analyse the particular job role, distilling out of the role all the aspects which are considered crucial to competence in the job.

In order to begin an analysis of the job role there are three distinct areas to focus on. First, there is performance. When we meet a competent person in this job role what could we expect them to be able to do? The first part of the analysis should ask what skills are needed and to what *level* of proficiency? Second, we need to ask what knowledge would we expect a competent person to retain. This knowledge should include an understanding of basic theories and concepts as well as more factual knowledge of the job, the organization and the industry. Finally, we need to ask what are the infrequent or unusual situations that the competent person would be expected to deal with? If this exercise is being carried out for a number of employees, it may be useful to produce a pro-forma, similar to that in Figure 2.5, but whichever way it is done, it should be

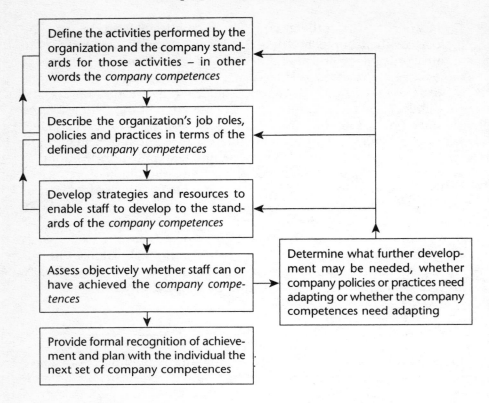

Figure 2.4 Defining company competences

done with employees that you believe are already competent. Producing a pro-forma for the employees to fill out individually could be very useful. It could be reasonably assumed that the issues raised by all the employees are likely to be the most crucial to competent performance.

Yet it is true that this analysis does not address some of the areas that were mentioned earlier, namely, basic numeracy, literacy, and a positive attitude to the success of themselves and the organization, interpersonal and social skills, and the confidence and the will to act. In terms of literacy and numeracy we may wish to use the achievement of existing qualifications such as GCSEs or Key Skills units to determine the level of these skills, but for some job roles these qualifications may be more demanding than what is absolutely necessary. (Key skills units are standards produced by QCA with equivalent core skills units produced by SQA in Scotland. For details, QCA and SQA can be contacted at the addresses in Appendix E.) What is certain is that when one carries out an analysis of the job role, numeracy, literacy and interpersonal and social skills will appear in some form or other if they are *crucial* to competent performance.

Job title

What should the competent person be able to do?

How well should they be able to do it?

What unusual situations would you expect the competent person to deal with?

What should the competent person know?

FACTS

THEORIES

How well should they know it?

Figure 2.5 The job skills inventory form

A positive attitude to the success of themselves and the organization, and the courage and will to act, may not be something which can be easily measured, although it may be deemed to be a significant part of competent performance. It is important to remember that we may be able to determine whether someone is competent in a particular job role by assessing their performance but ensuring that that person is enthusiastic and performing to (at least) that standard at all times, is a question of motivation and something which is more appropriately dealt with as part of ongoing management and supervision. Management support, encouragement, and the rewards offered to employees will all play a part in motivating the individual to perform at or above the standard.

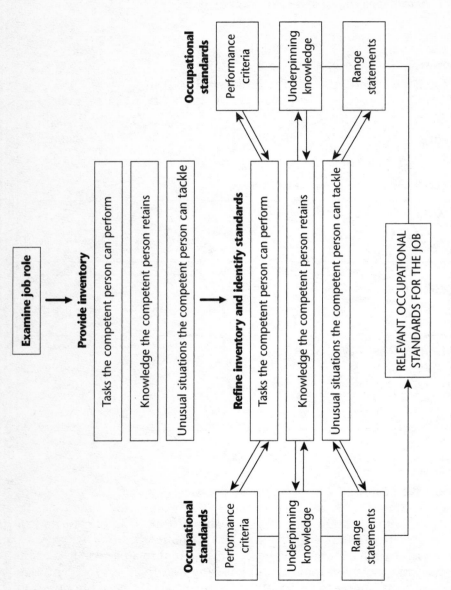

Figure 2.6 Identifying standards

After analysing the job role we are left with an inventory of the requirements of the job, a hotchpotch of skills knowledge and potential problem situations. The next stage is to examine the inventory, asking if all the areas described in the broad model of competence have been addressed. Finally, each item in the inventory should be rated as either crucial to competent performance or desirable for competent performance. This refined inventory can form the basis for a comparison between the job and relevant occupational standards. Occupational standards can then be selected for use with the assessment of competence (see Figure 2.6). Only at this stage can we look to adapt the occupational standards to better meet the organization and the individual's needs. Smaller organizations may find that it will not be worth the time and effort to adapt standards for a relatively small number of individuals.

Once the standards of competence have been determined for a particular job role they can be used as a basis for many functions including:

- recruitment and selection
- identification of training and development needs
- the evaluation of training and development activities
- the development of organizational systems and procedures.

3

SYSTEMS, PROCEDURES AND PRO-FORMAS

Summary

This chapter will look at:

- how competence standards can be used to help to focus the standard operating procedures for the organization

- the development of dynamic systems and procedures

- how evaluation and feedback routes allow for continual improvement

- show how occupational standards can help produce procedures, develop checklists, pro-formas, etc.

The application of national occupational standards in a work-place will often affect the systems and procedures of the organization. The standards may refer to systems and procedures which the organization either has not established or else the system and procedures are not agreed across the organization. Learning organizations will examine the standards to see how existing systems and procedures could be improved in line with the national standard.

USING THE COMPETENCY STANDARD

Once a standard has been developed for a particular function it has a variety of uses. It can be used as a mechanism to improve recruitment, personal development, performance appraisal, training, development and evaluation. In short, it is a tool for improving the performance of the individual and consequently of the organization. Of course, as with any tool it is only of benefit if it is used properly.

As mentioned previously, the power of standards of competence is that they can be measured. Measurement is the judging of an object in relation to a known object. In this case, the object for judging is an individual's performance and the known object is the occupational standard. If we use the driving test analogy again, it is easy to see that the performance of each learner driver is assessed by an examiner against set criteria. It is accepted that the learner driver is aware of the criteria and is ready to perform a number of manoeuvres and answer questions on command in order to demonstrate their competence. In a sense, all competency standards are predicated upon the same assumption, that the candidate, employee, trainee, or individual claiming competence, knows and believes that they can perform to the standard. It is their responsibility to prove to an assessor that this is in fact the case. Demonstrating their ability to the assessor is always the easiest way of proving competence.

Just as the driving examination system has evolved a particular procedure to maximize the effective assessment of the learner by the examiner, namely the UK driving test, it is possible to develop procedures and practices which will maximise the effectiveness of the assessment process for the individual and their assessor.

For many employers, an examination of the standards may point out a number of problems for their implementation. The standards may refer to systems and procedures that are not clear or even agreed within the organization. The first thing to remember is *don't panic:* one thing is certain, if the function is an important aspect of your work, then you will have systems and procedures in place already. It may be that those systems and procedures are very simple, informal, or even different depending on where the activity is performed or who performs it, but be sure it will exist. All that is required for a competence based approach is that these systems and procedures are agreed (not even that they are documented). It may be that the systems and procedures referred to in the standards are not agreed and they need to be developed further. However, if the organization has achieved or is working towards ISO 9000 certification (see Chapter 12), these systems and procedures will have to be documented.

SYSTEMS DESIGN

Systems and procedures that are imposed on organizations rarely survive. People need to discover how and why such systems are a benefit to the organization and themselves. When developing a system or procedure there are some useful rules:

1. *Always fully involve the individuals who are to operate the system.* The people who are to operate the system are in the best position to identify possible problems and identify solutions. If you are looking to further develop an existing system it may be that the operator designed the current system and what appears to you as idiosyncrasies

or peculiarities are in fact methods of addressing problems which you have not contemplated. Always remember that the operator is the systems expert.

2. *Ensure that the procedures are written in the language of the operators.* If procedures are to be read and used, they should be in a language and style of the user/operator. Ensure that the procedures are written in their own words and as simply as possible. Always write procedures in the active tense, use short sentences and avoid the use of absolutes such as 'never' or 'all the time,' where possible.

3. *Procedures must be written in a standard format where possible.* Yet the operator may need advice and guidance on how to write procedures to a standard format. The learning organization rests upon on the idea that everyone in the organization is responsible for and capable of innovation, everyone can and should contribute to the development of their own area of work and specifying the work procedures is the most basic level of this contribution.

4. *Always look at the simplest way with the fewest opportunities for human error.* Every step of a procedure which brings in another individual or another activity, brings in a further opportunity for an error. Any system is only as effective as the weakest link in the chain. However, the relationships to individuals in a system or procedure is important when analysing the opportunities for error. If ten people must *all* perform the same activity every day for the system to work then one error by one person will cause a system failure. If *any* of ten people perform the same activity every day for the system to work it would mean that it would need ten people to make the same error on the same day for a system failure.

5. *Always be prepared to adapt the system in the light of experience.* The purpose of any system or procedure is to assist the operator(s) to perform to the requirements of the organization. If it becomes clear that an adjustment to the systems or procedures will make them simpler or more effective, then the system should be changed with the minimum of fuss. Any failure of a system or procedure should prompt a review to examine why it failed and how the system can be adapted to prevent the same failure from happening again.

6. *Ensure wherever possible that the occupational standard is incorporated within the procedure.* Examine how the system or procedures can provide evidence of competence.

For an example of a procedure format see Figure 3.1, a procedure for providing clients with meals has been drawn up. In Figure 3.2 we can see how the procedure for one of the people involved in the procedure has been broken down into a more detailed procedure or set of instructions. One word of warning – developing systems and procedures is far simpler

PROCEDURE NUMBER	SS 011
PROCEDURE NAME	Providing clients with meals
OBJECTIVE	To ensure that all clients receive appropriate meals in accordance with their needs.
INVOLVING	Care Coordinator, Cook and Care Assistants
RELATES TO PROCEDURES	CC 112, C 2 & CA 010
Stage *Procedure*	

1.   COOK *(see C 2)*
Prepares all meals for clients. This will include breakfast, lunch and dinner.

Breakfast will normally be toast, cereal or a cooked breakfast. It will be provided as and when required during the hours of 7:30am and 11:00am.

Lunch and dinner will include a choice of drinks, and two choices of main meal and dessert. Lunch will be prepared for 1:00pm and dinner will be prepared for 5:30pm. Notification of choices will be provided by care staff a minimum of two hours before meal times.

Provides meals for clients where neither choice is acceptable.

Provides special dietary meals upon request.

Plans menu for four-week period in consultation with residents and suggests amendments to the menu.

2   CARE COORDINATOR *(see CC 112)*
Approves a four-weekly menu schedule for meals. Agrees any changes with the cook. Has responsibility for the control of the food budget.

3.   CARE ASSISTANT *(see CA 010)*
Helps clients prepare for their meal. Serves the meals assisting clients where necessary. Clears away dishes after the meal.

Date produced: 12/01/97   **Page 1 of 1**   **Version number 1**

Figure 3.1 Example of a procedure from a residential home

PROCEDURE NUMBER	CA 010
PROCEDURE NAME	Serving meals
OCCUPATIONAL STANDARD:	Z10 Enable clients to eat and drink (This is a unit from the care sector consortium standards.)
RESPONSIBILITY:	Care Assistant

1. At all times, the support given to clients will be consistent with their care plan.
2. The types of food offered to the client should only include items which are consistent with their care plan.
3. Each client is asked what they would like to eat and drink from the selection on offer.
4. The different options are explained if necessary, to help the client make a choice.
5. Where possible, the client is offered an alternative if they don't like what is on offer.
6. Record each choice on the meal list (form MM12) and pass to cook at least two hours before the meal time.
7. Each client is asked where they would like to eat their meal.
8. Each client is helped to wash their hands, find a comfortable seating position and is given appropriate eating and drinking utensils and a napkin.
9. When clients are presented with their food, they are offered condiments and help with feeding themselves if appropriate.
10. All clients are monitored during the meal and offered support if necessary.
11. Where requested, a clients intake is recorded on the daily intake form (Form MM18).
12. The fact that a client did not eat is recorded on their daily report sheet (Form DD7) along with any known or suspected reason.
13. If a client misses two meals or is causing concern, it is reported to senior staff as a matter of urgency.

Figure 3.2 Example of how the procedure can produce work instructions

than implementing them. If they cannot be implemented then do not develop them. If the organization either is or wishes to become ISO 9000 registered, then all procedures must be demonstrated to be operating effectively. Always try to focus on the outcomes of the procedure, ie, what is the procedure trying to achieve. Often, simply analysing the organizations systems will identify many pointless or redundant procedures.

THE USE OF PRO-FORMAS

In order to prove competence to a particular standard, the individual needs to provide evidence of their competence to the person who is to make the judgement (in NVQ terms, that person is the assessor). Standardized materials can assist the production of good quality evidence of an individual's competence. The scope for such materials seems infinite, but these materials are best produced only where their use will assist an individual in the day to day operation of their function or job role and not simply to meet the evidence requirements. If the use of a pro-forma or checklist is likely to make the performance of the job more difficult, more time consuming, then nine times out of ten, there will be other ways of producing the evidence which will be more appropriate.

If we take the Blackbird Productions example one stage further we can see how a simple pro-forma can help the employee meet the requirements of the organization, the requirements of the standards *and* produce good quality evidence at the same time. First of all we need to take the adapted standard and see what products are generated naturally in the work-place by the individual performing this function (see Figure 2.3). For Blackbird Productions the key documents will be a *conference proposal report* and a *contractor's tender invitation*. Both of these documents are produced by the individuals who are to be the candidates and both are produced on word processors. The way that most of these reports are produced is by using previous reports as a basis. Although this has been a satisfactory way of producing reports, not all reports would clearly demonstrate all the performance criteria had been met in every instance. Any units or elements which require the production of reports are ideal for developing pro-formas or templates. The conference proposal report for Blackbird Productions could be produced from a template, similar to that in Figure 3.3. The template would form the basis of each report. Each section that has italicized text within brackets would be written by the author of the report. The italicized text describes what the author needs to cover. After each section, where appropriate, the performance criteria that the section is addressing has been indicated.

The production of this conference proposal report should provide good evidence of competence to fully meet all the performance criteria except (g), (h) and (j). Of these outstanding criteria, the requirements of (g) will be met if the conference proposal committee and the client approve the report, (h) will be specified in the contractor's tender invitation and the requirements of (i) will be met through using the agreed templates of the conference proposal report and the contractor's tender invitation.

The contractor's tender invitation could be produced by using a template which borrows from the conference proposal report and should include a portion of the former document. This in effect would mean that the

---

Conference proposal report

- **A proposal for a conference on** *subject area* **by Blackbird Productions on behalf of** *client name.*

- **Background**

  Cover the recent history of the relationship between BP and the client, including any recent collaborative projects

- **The** *client name/subject area* **conference**

  Include the proposed title of the conference

  Outline the aims and objectives of the conference **pc (a)**

  Outline the key tasks involved in staging the conference, including a proposed time-scale and any deadlines envisaged **pcs (e) and (f)**

  Outline the progress reporting procedure and the proposed evaluation criteria for the conference **pc (i)**

- **The value of the conference**

  Include the significance and value of the conference to BP and the client **pc (b)**

  Include any links between the client's policies or current activities and the proposed conference **pc (c)**

- **The outcomes of the conference**

  Include all the possible benefits to the client of running the conference and list all the outcomes such as sales, contacts, product/brand awareness, etc and how these benefits can be used by the client to gain a competitive advantage **pc (d)**

- **The resources required/available**

  Outline the contribution of BP, the client and proposed contractor involvement

  Assess the conference costs and their relationship to the client's budget where possible

Note: PC = performance criteria

Figure 3.3 Conference proposal report

tender invitation would be partly a 'cut and paste' exercise (if using a word-processor, it may be worthwhile to actually link sections of the contractor's tender invitation with the conference proposal report using the latter as the source document). The contractor's tender invitation could then look something like Figure 3.4.

The production of these two documents for staff of Blackbird Productions would mean that they would meet all their normal work requirements consistently, efficiently and effectively *and in the process*, provide good quality performance evidence of all the performance criteria across the range of appropriate documents. Moreover, assuming that clients and contractors are external to the organization, the candidate is only looking for evidence in relation to sole traders and volunteers to complete the range of clients and contractors.

These two pro-formas have been developed to address the requirements of one particular element from the Museum Training Institute's standards. Yet the fictitious Blackbird Productions could operate across a whole gamut of occupational standards which could include management (Management Charter Initiative – MCI), administration (Administration Standards Council – ASC), design (Design Lead Body – DLB), marketing (Marketing Lead Body – MLB), among many. It would therefore make sense to examine other relevant standards and see how the pro-formas could be written to address the evidence requirements of other elements of other standards. For example, these two pro-formas could be integrated with procedures which would ensure that they would address the evidence requirements of unit C8 Select personnel for activities from the MCI's standards. (The MCI standards have incorporated the items of range within the evidence requirements and therefore, an exposition of the performance criteria alongside the evidence requirements should provide us with all we need to determine what is needed to produce good quality performance evidence.) If we look at the key elements of C8.1 Identify personnel requirements (Figure 3.5) and C8.2 Select required personnel (Figure 3.6) we can see how these two documents could form evidence of the achievement of that particular unit.

First we need to adapt the MCI standard for use by Blackbird Productions' staff (see Figures 3.7 and 3.8).

Both the project proposal (see Figure 3.3 – with the addition of an extra point under *Resources required/available* – 'include the organizational objectives and constraints in employing contractors' pc (g)) and the contractor's tender invitation (see Figure 3.4) could provide evidence of element C8.1.

The project proposal could provide evidence of pc (a), the contractor's tender invitation could provide evidence of pcs (c), (d) and (e). Evidence that the learner has consulted with the appropriate people on the development of the contractor's tender invitation and that the final version has

---

Contractor's tender invitation

- *Contractor's name* **is invited to tender for the work outline below by Blackbird Productions on behalf of** *client name.*

- **Background**

  Cover the recent history of the relationship between BP and the client, including any recent collaborative projects

- **The** *client name/subject area* **conference**

  Include the proposed title of the conference

  Outline the aims and objectives of the conference

  Outline the key tasks involved in staging the conference, including a proposed time-scale and any deadlines envisaged

- **The resources required/available**

  Outline the main contribution of BP, the client and proposed contractor involvement

- **Tender details**

  Outline the area of work or the services to be provided by the contractor

  Specify the work / services. Include all deadlines, any constraints upon working time, access to the site and any prescribed working practices or materials

  Outline the criteria upon which the work will be evaluated, including any penalties

- **Format of tender**

  Outline documentation required, such as quotes, referees, examples of work

  State the deadline for the receipt of tenders

- **Selection criteria pc (h)**

  Outline the criteria upon which the tenders will be evaluated

  Outline the stages of the selection process, stating the date when a decision will be made, and a date by which the unsuccessful bidders will be notified

Note: Sections in italics are completed by the person extending the invitation

Figure 3.4 Contractor's tender invitation

Unit C8 Select personnel for activities

ELEMENT C8.1 Identify personnel requirements

PERFORMANCE CRITERIA

You must ensure that

(a) You clearly and accurately identify the organizational objectives and constraints affecting *personnel* requirements.

(b) You consult with people on *personnel* requirements in a timely and confidential manner.

(c) Your estimates of personnel requirements are based on an accurate analysis of sufficient, up-to-date and reliable information.

(d) The *specifications* you develop are clear, accurate and comply with organizational and legal requirements.

(e) The *specifications* you develop identify fair and objective criteria for selection.

(f) The *specifications* you develop are agreed with *authorized people* prior to recruitment action.

EVIDENCE REQUIREMENTS

You must prove that you *identify personnel requirements* to the National Standard of Competence.
To do this, you must provide evidence to convince your assessor that you consistently meet *all* the performance criteria.
Your evidence must be the result of real work activities undertaken by yourself. Evidence from simulated activities is *not* acceptable for this element.
You must show evidence that you identify requirements for at least *four* of the following types of *personnel*:

- internal
- external
- permanent
- temporary
- full-time
- part-time
- paid
- voluntary

You must also show evidence that you involve at least *two* of the following types of *authorized people*:

- team members
- colleagues working at the same level as yourself
- higher-level managers or sponsors
- personnel specialists
- members of the selection team

You must also show that you develop *all* of the following types of specifications:

- key purpose of the posts
- individual and team roles and responsibilities
- required individual and team competencies
- other details specific to the organization.

You must, however, convince your assessor that you have the necessary knowledge, understanding and skills to be able to perform competently in respect of *all* types of *personnel* and *authorized people*, listed above.

Figure 3.5 MCI version of element C8.1: identify personnel requirements

Unit C8 Select personnel for activities

ELEMENT C8.2 Select required personnel

PERFORMANCE CRITERIA

You must ensure that

(a) You use appropriately skilled and experienced people to assess and select *personnel*.

(b) The *information* you obtain about each candidate is relevant to and sufficient for the selection process.

(c) You assess the *information* objectively against specified selection criteria.

(d) Your selection decisions are justifiable from the evidence gained.

(e) You only inform authorized people about selection decisions and the identified development needs of successful candidates.

(f) The information you provide to authorized people is clear and accurate.

(g) All candidates receive feedback and information appropriate to their needs at each stage of the selection process.

(h) Your records of the selection process are complete, accurate, clear and comply with organizational and legal requirements.

(i) You pass on your recommendations for improvements to the selection process to the appropriate people in your organization.

EVIDENCE REQUIREMENTS

You must prove that you *select required personnel* to the National Standard of Competence.
To do this, you must provide evidence to convince your assessor that you consistently meet *all* the performance criteria.
Your evidence must be the result of real work activities undertaken by yourself. Evidence from simulated activities is *not* acceptable for this element.
You must show evidence that you identify requirements for at least *four* of the following types of *personnel*:
- internal
- external
- permanent
- temporary
- full-time
- part-time
- paid
- voluntary

You must also show evidence that you obtain and assess at least *four* of the following types of *information*:
- biographical data
- letters
- references
- interview responses
- presentations
- results of work skill tests
- results of knowledge tests.

You must, however, convince your assessor that you have the necessary knowledge, understanding and skills to be able to perform competently in respect of *all* types of *personnel* and *information*, listed above.

Figure 3.6 MCI version of element C8.2: select required personnel

Unit C8 Select personnel for activities

ELEMENT C8.1 Identify contractor requirements

PERFORMANCE CRITERIA

You must ensure that

(a) You clearly and accurately identify the organizational objectives and constraints affecting *contractors'* requirements.

(b) You consult with people on *contractors'* requirements in a timely and confidential manner.

(c) Your estimates of contractors requirements are based on an accurate analysis of sufficient, up-to-date and reliable information.

(d) The *tender document's selection criteria* you develop are clear, accurate and comply with organizational and legal requirements.

(e) The *tender document's selection criteria* you develop identify fair and objective criteria for selection.

(f) The *tender document's selection criteria* you develop are agreed with *authorized people* prior to recruitment action.

EVIDENCE REQUIREMENTS

You must prove that you *identify personnel requirements* to the National Standard of Competence.
To do this, you must provide evidence to convince your assessor that you consistently meet *all* the performance criteria. Your evidence must be the result of real work activities undertaken by yourself. Evidence from simulated activities is *not* acceptable for this element.
You must show evidence that you identify requirements for all the following types of *contractor*:
• external   • full-time
• temporary   • paid
You must also show evidence that you involve at least *two* of the following types of *authorized people*:
• team members
• higher-level managers or sponsors
You must also show that you develop *all* of the following types of selection criteria:
• key purpose of the posts
• individual and team roles and responsibilities
• required individual and team competencies
• other details specific to the organization.
You must, however, convince your assessor that you have the necessary knowledge, understanding and skills to be able to perform competently in respect of the following types of *contractor*:
• internal   • part-time
• permanent   • voluntary
and the following types of *authorized people*:
• colleagues working at the same level as yourself
• personnel specialists
• members of the selection team.

Figure 3.7 Blackbird Productions' version of element C8.1: identify contractor requirements

Unit C8 Select personnel for activities

ELEMENT C8.2 Select required contractor

PERFORMANCE CRITERIA

You must ensure that

(a) You use appropriately skilled and experienced people to assess and select *contractor*.

(b) The *information* you obtain about each candidate is relevant to and sufficient for the selection process.

(c) You assess the *information* objectively against specified selection criteria.

(d) Your selection decisions are justifiable from the evidence gained.

(e) You only inform authorized people about selection decisions and the identified development needs of successful contractors.

(f) The information you provide to authorized people is clear and accurate.

(g) All contractors receive feedback and information appropriate to their needs at each stage of the selection process.

(h) Your records of the selection process are complete, accurate, clear and comply with organizational and legal requirements.

(i) You pass on your recommendations for improvements to the selection process to the appropriate people in your organization.

EVIDENCE REQUIREMENTS

You must prove that you *select required personnel* to the National Standard of Competence.
To do this, you must provide evidence to convince your assessor that you consistently meet *all* the performance criteria.
Your evidence must be the result of real work activities undertaken by yourself. Evidence from simulated activities is *not* acceptable for this element.
You must show evidence that you identify requirements for all the following types of *contractor*:
● external
● temporary
● full-time
● paid
You must also show evidence that you obtain and assess all the following types of *information*:
● biographical data
● letters
● references
● interview responses
You must, however, convince your assessor that you have the necessary knowledge, understanding and skills to be able to perform competently in respect of the following types of *contractor*:
● internal   ● part-time
● permanent   ● voluntary
and the following types of *information*:
● presentations
● results of work skill tests
● results of knowledge tests.

Figure 3.8 Blackbird Productions' version of element C8.2: select required contractor

been agreed with authorized people, prior to the tender being distributed should satisfy the requirements of criteria (b) and (f).

Element C8.2 relates to the process of selecting the contractor based on the information supplied by the prospective contractors. An agreed process for the learner to follow could address all the performance criteria of element C8.2.

Standard operating procedures

Many organizations have developed standard operating procedures, especially in environments where mistakes can be very costly. Standard operating procedures describe the way in which the organizations' employees should operate. Unlike competence statements that refer to the outcomes of performance, standard procedures look to standardize just how those outcomes are achieved. They will describe a way of performing, or a set of steps to follow. Often, situations will call for standard operating procedures to ensure that consistency is achieved.

Most organizations have some standard operating procedures. For many organizations these are not documented but simply passed from one operative to the next through an informal system. Although simple, this does not ensure that all information is passed on, often a small piece of vital information is forgotten, leading to inefficiencies. Indeed, it may not be worthwhile going to all the trouble of determining standard operating procedures for many of the tasks undertaken in an organization, as the value of standard operating procedures must be measured against the effort involved in defining, agreeing monitoring and reviewing the application of such procedures.

Nevertheless, standard operating procedures can be extremely beneficial in structuring the way in which individuals approach a task and demonstrate their competence. Indeed, there are many situations where standard procedures are crucially important, including appraisal and induction systems.

The benefit of standard operating procedures is that they provide consistency, but at a cost to the individual's ability to innovate. Standard operating procedures mitigate against individuals developing new and different ways of operating. It checks the ability of individuals to develop ways of working that suit their strengths and abilities.

Feedback loops

To address the problem of restricted opportunities for innovation in the activity, standard operating procedures need to be under continual review.

If improvements are identified there should be a system which will identify and implement change. This will provide the benefits of standard operating procedures but allow opportunities for change and innovation.

The organization may be ISO 9000 registered, if it is, it will have a systems and procedures manual which will describe all the systems and procedures operated in the organization, including the system for amending systems and procedures.

4

JOB DESCRIPTIONS AND APPRAISAL SYSTEMS

Summary

In this chapter you will learn about:

- how competence standards help to produce accurate job descriptions
- how competence standards can form a basis of an appraisal system.

Once the standards of performance for a particular post have been identified they can be used as a basis for the selection process, they can be specified in the job description and finally used as a measure of ongoing performance as part of the appraisal process. This should ensure consistency and a system of internal validation to the process of selection and appraisal. Consequently, changes to the standards at one part of the process should point to changes at other parts. If, for example, it is decided that one particular standard is not relevant to assess ongoing performance, should not that same standard be dropped from the job description or the job specification. Ensuring that such a feedback loop is operating is often a good way of further refining a large list of competencies to a more reasonable working list of the most critical competencies.

COMPETENCE-BASED JOB DESCRIPTIONS

A job description is simply a way of illustrating the purpose, duties, authority and responsibility of the job-holder, and as such act as the key terms of reference for an employee. As a description of a job role it should change as that job role changes, always keeping pace with the changing nature of the industry and requirements of the employer. Unfortunately, not much use is made of job descriptions, possibly because they are not written in a way that would make them particularly useful. Though a more likely reason is that individuals are not always keen to be made accountable for their actions by having an agreed job description, often it suits them to be a little bit hazy about what exactly is required of them. Indeed, this often suits employers who do not like the thought that an employee will turn around and say 'Sorry, but that is not my job' (this fear often leads to the 'anything else' line at the end of many job descriptions. Where one of the responsibilities is to perform any duty deemed necessary by their manager, thereby at a stroke negating the whole concept of the job description).

Hence, job descriptions are not very specific, making quite broad statements which are then left open to a wide variety of interpretations. However, the job description could be utilized as one of the most important communication mediums available to organizations if they were to accurately reflect the changing nature and demands of the job role. Therefore, they are always open to review.

In order to make maximum use of the job description it should not only describe what needs to be done but the standard to which it should be done.

Design

The typical job description should include a number of common sections.

- Job information such as job title, grade, department, and possibly, location, hours and holiday entitlement.
- Lines of communication such as who she is responsible to and who she is responsible for.
- Role statement, a broad description of the nature and purpose of the job, often in the form of aims and objectives.
- Activity statement, a list of the main tasks or duties the post-holder will be required to perform.
- Competence statement, a list of the standards to which the tasks should be performed.
- Other information, could include information on the working conditions, any legal requirements which pertain to the job, even information about the culture of the organization.

When constructed, the job description should provide a brief but accurate description of what is required of the post-holder. A good job description ensures that an individual and their employer have the same understanding of what is required of the post.

The use of occupational standards enables individuals to assess their own suitability for the position and enables them to ascertain the exact standard of performance required, something which would not be possible from the list of activities.

> ### **Remember**
>
> Competence-based job descriptions which accurately describe the training and development responsibility of employees should be good evidence towards IiP indicators 1.3 and 2.5 (Chapter 10). Competence-based job descriptions which outline the assessment or verification responsibilities of employees should be good evidence towards approved centre criteria 1.1.3 (Chapter 11).

APPRAISAL SYSTEMS

Once an organization has recruited an individual to a post and both the individual and the employer understand the requirements of the post, as described in an accurate job description, the next stage for the organization (after the induction and initial training) is to monitor and support that individual to achieve their full potential in the job role. An appraisal process can assist in providing this support, providing a structure for the formal discussion of issues around the development of the post-holder and the job.

Many organizations have appraisal schemes although they have often acquired euphemistic titles such as 'performance review', 'development interview', 'work planning interview', etc. Indeed, the quality and effectiveness of the appraisal system is about as varied as the titles used. Whatever the title, an appraisal system is a crucial part of organizational communication and as such, an effective appraisal system is central to the operation of a learning organization. For if learning is to occur, there needs to be good quality information available upon which action can be taken to address problems of performance and plan the development of learners, allowing the organization to learn. It could be argued that a learning organization where managers and supervisors discuss perform-ance and agree corrective and developmental actions on a regular and informal way indicates there is no need for a structured appraisal system. In theory such organizations should exist but in practice they are extremely rare.

The controversy and unease that surrounds some appraisal systems is no more than an expression of the issues that surround any assessment. In the case of appraisals this is amplified by the direct relationship between the assessment decision and the career prospects of the appraisee.

Appraisal systems usually have many objectives, Clive Fletcher (1993) identifies a number:

- making reward decisions
- improving performance
- motivating staff
- succession planning and identifying potential
- promoting manager/subordinate dialogue
- eradicating unsatisfactory performance.

Although all these objectives are worthy, the main aim for a learning organization is to improve performance on both an individual and organizational level. An effective appraisal system should accurately assess performance and provide the appraisee with the information and motivation to improve and develop their competence.

Objectivity

The primary objection to appraisal systems is that they involve a degree of subjectivity by the appraiser. This is a fact of all appraisal systems, just as it is a fact of all assessment systems. Rather than ignore these concerns we should acknowledge that this is a natural part of all appraisal systems and we should attempt to quantify the degree of subjectivity that could colour the outcome of the appraisal.

In trying to determine an accurate and objective system of appraisal we should recognize that what could be described as a very personal and subjective description of an employee's performance by a manager or a supervisor is not necessarily inaccurate. Simply because an employee does not recognize themselves in the appraisal does not mean that it is not accurate. If the manager believes that the appraisal is accurate then it does have some validity because it is how the manager experiences the performance of that particular individual. However, if our primary aim is to motivate the individual to improve their performance, what we need to do is to assist the appraiser and appraisee to arrive at a common understanding of what is an accurate description of performance.

All appraisal systems will differ and there is no ideal or universal appraisal system which will be effective in all organizations. All appraisal systems will differ in terms of structure, frequency and the level of formality dependent upon the needs of the organization.

Most organizations rely on the instruments of the system (the forms, the procedures) to provide objective and accurate appraisals even though any individual's experience of the appraisal system is determined mainly upon the skills, abilities and attitude of the appraiser. For example, the feedback from an appraiser could motivate the appraisee to improve their performance, yet the same information presented differently could lead to the appraisee being de-motivated. Clearly the training, development and support of appraisers is vital to the success of any appraisal system.

Developing an appraisal system

The simple or traditional model of appraisal consisting of the line manager as appraiser and the subordinate as appraisee is no longer practicable for many organizations. Consequently, the structure of the organization's management systems will determine, to some degree, the type of appraisal system that is developed.

The questions that need to be asked are:

1. *Who should be the appraiser?* Does the appraisee have a line manager who has enough contact to justify being the main source of the appraisal or does the appraisee have a number of managers, all of whom could provide an input into the appraisal? There could be other employees who could provide input into the performance appraisal who may not have a management responsibility. Identifying the appraisers is the first step.
2. *Where can self-appraisal be used?* Self-appraisal is extremely useful in providing a more balanced picture of performance. Research has demonstrated that individuals are relatively good at assessing their own performance. It is unlikely that organizations will rely on self-appraisal on its own, usually self-appraisal is used to support and complement the judgement of other appraisers and importantly to help nurture ownership of the process in the appraisee.
3. *Should there be a number of appraisers?* Using a number of appraisal sources may be more complicated in terms of coordination, however, any possible prejudice or bias is minimized.
4. *What should be the frequency of the appraisal?* This may be dependent upon the opportunities available to the appraiser(s) and appraisee to meet. It may also depend to some extent on the content of the appraisal itself.

Planning and design

Planning

- Draw up an appraisal plan of all employees based upon the organizational chart.
- Link all employees to their appraiser(s), briefly explain the reason for appointing the appraiser for each individual, add up the total expected hours of appraisal and review required of each appraiser.

- A schedule of training and development should be drawn up to ensure that all appraisers understand and develop the skills required to participate effectively in the new system.
- Discuss the proposed allocation of appraisal responsibilities with appraisers and appraisees.
- Adjust the system based upon the feedback from participants.
- Communicate the aims and objectives of the appraisal system to all.

Design – content

- For each post there should be standards.
- For each individual there should also be goals. The nature of the individuals and their posts will determine the balance between goals and standards.
- The standards should be based on competence standards determined for the individual such as those described in Chapter 2.
- The appraisal may be on a scheduled sampling basis so that over a period of time (preferably not more than three years) all the selected standards are assessed.
- The goals should be measurable and based upon the timetable of the appraisal system. Where the individual has goals which span periods of time which are outside the appraisal review timetable, milestones towards the goal should be determined.
- The appraisal system looks backwards, not just forward. Therefore, the appraisal system must look at what was achieved since the last appraisal. Where the goals were not achieved, the appraiser and the appraisee need to determine why. They also need to plan how these goals can be achieved this coming year or else set new, realistic goals.
- The appraisal system should assist in the process of identifying and agreeing the appraisee's training and development needs. The appraisee should be involved in determining their learning needs with the appraiser responsible for advising and guiding the appraisee.
- The appraisal should look at the impact of any learning activity that has taken place in the previous appraisal period.

Design – assessment process

If the occupational standards used in the appraisal process are to be assessed by NVQ or SVQ assessors there need be no further work in defining the assessment process. However, if the standards are to be assessed outside the quality assurance framework provided by an awarding body, an acceptable level of evidence needs to be determined for the appraiser and appraisee.

Just as the occupational standards can be adapted to fit the needs of the organization, the evidence requirements or evidence specifications can also be adapted to fit the needs of the appraisal system.

The evidence requirements or specification of the occupational standards are usually written to allow a great degree of flexibility in the nature of the evidence that is needed for each element. The scope of the evidence requirements is designed to ensure performance in a range of organizations, something your organization may not be as concerned with. The evidence requirements also usually specify the level of performance evidence required, the critical areas of range and the amount of evidence required.

For the purposes of appraisal it may be that 'the burden of proof' is less than that required of an NVQ awarding body (alternatively it may be that the organization requires a greater level of evidence than that outlined by the awarding bodies). It may also be seen as useful to be far more prescriptive about the nature of the evidence rather than leaving it entirely up to the individual being assessed. The organization may also wish to discard some of the range statements, or knowledge specifications to make them more organizationally relevant.

The assessment of the standards can be used as a key method of ongoing review and monitoring of performance, so that the actual appraisal interview serves to document the assessment outcomes rather than form a part of the actual assessment process. Yet appraisal does involve the assessment of performance and as such relies on the appraiser having assessment skills covered in the next chapter.

Evaluation

A simple way to evaluate the appraisal process and help the organization to learn from the experiences of individuals that operate it, is to gather raw data through simple post-appraisal questionnaires. The objectives of the evaluation would be to ascertain the appraisee and the appraiser's experience of the process, and to register any insights gained from the experience. As already mentioned, evaluation is a critical part of any learning organization, it is not simply a process of sending out questionnaires. The questionnaire can only provide the raw data, the evaluation comes from the critical analysis of that data.

In constructing the questionnaire it is important to keep in mind what information we want from participants. The organization may want to find out:

- how long the whole process took
- if the process matched their expectations
- if they were sufficiently prepared for the process
- if the goals or standards were reasonable
- if the process pointed to deficiencies in other areas such as job descriptions
- if the process was enjoyable or not

- are there comments that the recipient would wish to pass on about the process, which was not covered in the questionnaire.

Once we have identified the key areas we wish to explore, we can then carefully construct focused (not loaded) questions to extract the participants' views.

Remember

An effective appraisal system can provide good quality evidence of IiP indicators 1.3, 2.3, 2.6, 3.2, 3.3, 3.4, 3.5, 3.6, 4.1, 4.2 (Chapter 10).

5

ASSESSING PERFORMANCE

Summary

This chapter will look at:

- the assessment of performance
- types of evidence
- judging evidence
- recording judgements.

ASSESSMENT OF COMPETENCE

Assessment of performance, of someone's competence, is central to all development activities. If the occupational standard is the tool then assessment is the most obvious use of that tool. Before we can identify the development that is needed by a learner, an assessment of the current competence is made. Before we can select an individual for a post, an assessment of their current competence is made. Before we can evaluate the effectiveness of a particular training activity, an assessment of the current competence is made. Thus, if the occupational standard is the mechanism that is used consistently across human resource development (HRD) functions, it makes sense to ensure that the assessment of the occupational standard is consistent across all those functions.

What is meant by assessing performance?

Assessment is something we all do, indeed we could say that we are almost obsessional about it. We naturally assess other people in all situations, often forming quite erroneous views about others. For as long as this remains an unconscious activity during informal situations we all tolerate it and hope that others don't make unfavourable assessments of ourselves. However, when assessments are formal and will lead to rewards of some kind, our view is somewhat different. Although we may tolerate inaccurate assessments if they are in our favour, we feel that we should be accurately assessed. In this situation, *accurate* is used to mean *agreed* between the assessor and the learner.

If learners are to maximize their learning potential it is essential that they are able to assess their performance. This will enable them to identify where shortcomings may exist and plan learning activities to address those shortcomings.

Understanding performance

The first step in assessing performance for any learner is recognizing what constitutes acceptable performance. For some activities this may seem very straightforward, we may see others performing the particular task in question and feel that this provides us with enough information to determine what is acceptable performance. However, if we take a very simple skill, one which many of us learn at an early age such as riding a bike, we can see in Table 5.1 how our appreciation of what is acceptable performance develops during the learning process.

For most of us, to understand what constitutes acceptable performance is something that develops as our abilities and competence develop. As we start on the road to acquiring any particular skill or ability, our understanding of it is refined and honed, becoming more and more sophisticated. Often our initial understanding of what is acceptable performance is, in hindsight, laughably simplistic. Often people will quite honestly believe that they can function to a particular standard, because they believe that the unit title describes what they do. It is only when they read the details of the unit that they begin to realize that they do not perform to that standard. Furthermore, since occupational standards have been developed by competent practitioners *for* competent practitioners, they are not designed to be necessarily understood by non-practitioners. They are, in a sense, often written in the language of the work-place, and may include many words which have a specific or extended meaning in that industry or sector.

Until we have an accurate understanding of what acceptable performance is, we cannot measure ourselves against it. That in a sense is the hard part, once performance has been accurately defined, determining whether or not someone has met the performance is relatively easy as long as the definition is written in terms which are measurable outcomes. This means that to describe performance in these terms we have to be far more specific than what we are used to. The great advantage that occupational standards provide for us is that those very detailed, specific

Table 5.1 How our appreciation develops during the learning process

Stages in understanding how to ride a bike	Learning activities
Watch someone ride a bike.	Identify what constitutes performance through observation.
Try to balance on the bike and propel oneself forward at the same time (remember how absolutely impossible this seemed at your first attempt).	Practise cycling by mimicking the actions of a cyclist. Attempt performance.
Realize that standing watching someone ride a bike from the safety and security of having both feet planted firmly on the ground is very different from the view in the saddle.	Identify what constitutes performance through experience and observation. The understanding of what constitutes performance is reassessed.
Suddenly realize that what appeared to be a very minor skill, the ability to stop, has found a new and very urgent importance.	Identify what constitutes performance through improving on one's own observation skills. The understanding of what constitutes performance is reassessed.
Having mastered the skills of moving forward, balancing and stopping, one can then proceed to the next level of cycling proficiency such as turning corners, riding in traffic, obeying and understanding road safety signals.	Identify what constitutes performance through experience and observation. The understanding of what constitutes performance is reassessed.
Without further study to gain the knowledge of the highway code a cyclist could not reasonably be deemed to be competent.	Research what constitutes the rules and regulations which govern the safe use of cycles on public highways.

measurements of performance have been developed, consequently making it remarkably easy to assess competence.

Impartiality in assessment

The skills of assessment are skills which are useful for all members of a learning organization, not simply reserved for appraisers or assessors. In fact, it could be said that all members of learning organizations need to be appraisers or assessors. The main skills of assessment include:

- impartiality
- attention to detail
- effective planning and organization
- inter-personal skills such as listening, counselling, giving feedback, and motivating.

Most of these skills are well covered in training and development publications so they are not revisited here. However, one skill that is crucial to assessment is impartiality or objectivity. Whether the assessment of performance is for the purpose of recruitment and selection, identifying training needs, appraisal, a skills audit, an SVQ or NVQ, the person performing the assessment must remain impartial.

First, I must begin by saying that a completely objective assessment is an unrealistic goal, what we are looking to achieve is the most impartial assessment possible. This means one where the assessor has made a judgement based on the evidence alone and both her and the learner feel that it is an accurate assessment.

To ensure that the climate is conducive to an impartial assessment the organization needs to ensure that pressures are not placed upon the person making the assessment which may encourage a particular outcome. These pressures could include conflicting responsibilities, for instance, where the assessor is responsible for reducing the salary budget but at the same time, the results of her assessment will affect performance related pay increases. Such situations can only undermine the whole process, as even the most impartial of assessors will be tempted or at least seen as such by unhappy appraisees.

Table 5.2 is a list of some of the key pitfalls of the inexperienced assessor. The first step to eradicating bias is to recognize how it can occur. All these errors can be overcome from using occupational standards as the *only* measurement of performance.

Table 5.2 Some of the key pitfalls of the inexperienced assessor

The halo effect	This is where the assessor allows some attractive or favourable aspects of the learner's performance to colour their view of other less favourable aspects. This is also possible in reverse where negative aspects colour one's views, sometimes known as the 'horns effect'.
Judgement based on exceptional events	Where the performance is judged on the exceptional events, when the learner's activities have attracted wide attention. Usually costly errors or praiseworthy actions, either way, these are not usually a good measure of overall performance. These exceptional events will tend to colour the assessor's view and are a result of a lack of direct contact with the learners.
'Just like me'	Where the learner demonstrates a similarity in personality, attitudes or background and the assessor responds positively to these attractive traits.
Judgements based on erroneous beliefs	We all hold erroneous beliefs based often on stereotyping or our unproved personal theories of personality. We often believe that certain types of people will behave in certain ways. Most of the time there is no rational foundation for these theories but they can colour our judgements.
Judgements which ignore the context	There is a danger that the ability of a learner to affect the course of events is overstated. Sometimes this is encouraged by the learner because it will make them and their abilities appear more significant than they actually are. The assessor must make a judgement as to the contribution of the learner.

EVIDENCE

For an assessor to judge the evidence, that evidence needs to be produced and collected. This could be done by the assessor or the learner. Usually it will be a mixture of both but the main input will be from the learner. It makes sense that the learner who has most to gain from the experience (and the one who is most familiar with the actual activities and performance undertaken) is given the responsibility for producing and generating the evidence. In other words, the responsibility for proving they are competent resides with the learner.

If we are asking learners to prove to assessors that they are competent it seems only fair that we should allow them to bring forward anything they wish as evidence. Yet this does not mean that anything put forward as evidence would be deemed acceptable or relevant by the assessor. The assessor must judge each item of evidence on its own merits. Each piece of evidence must be critically and rigorously assessed. The key questions that an assessor should ask of *every* piece of evidence are:

- Is it relevant? Does the evidence prove that this learner has performed to the required standard? Does the evidence directly demonstrate this?
- Is it authentic? Is this evidence of this learner's performance and not someone else's? If it is evidence produced by a team, is it clear the extent of the learner's contribution?
- Is it reliable? Would other assessors faced with the same evidence come to the same conclusion?
- Is it current? Does the evidence demonstrate that the learner can perform the activity at the time of the assessment?

The strength of all of the evidence presented needs to be judged by the assessor to determine whether or not that particular learner has proved that she can consistently perform to the standard.

Performance evidence

The assessment of competence is the assessment of someone's ability to perform in a real working environment, therefore the type of evidence must be one that reflects that performance. The assessor then needs to look for evidence of performance or performance evidence. The main types of performance evidence are:

- a demonstration of the activity by the learner
- products of the learner's work
- testimony of a credible witness that they have observed the learner performing to the standard
- a demonstration by the learner during a simulation of the activity.

Occupational standards will relate to all the types of activities undertaken in organizations. Routine and non-routine activities which take a short time to complete and others which may take a long time. Obviously, some forms of evidence will always be more reliable than others and for this reason it is always useful to try and target the most appropriate evidence. For the most efficient assessment it is important to match the type of evidence with the activity. If an activity to be assessed takes a short time to complete and it occurs on a predictable basis it will be an ideal activity for the assessor to observe. An assessor observing a learner demonstrating their performance to the standard will always be the preferred form of evidence and should be used where possible. However, this is not always possible because, either the activity takes a long time to complete, or it is not possible to predict occurrences of the activity. The flowchart in Figure 5.1 will direct the learner to the most appropriate and best quality evidence. Although, in order to gain *full* coverage of the entire standard or to demonstrate that the standard has been met consistently over time, a number of different types of evidence may be used.

Knowledge evidence

Performance evidence is the primary source for judging the learner's competence. However, performance evidence alone could not provide us with a confirmation that the learner has the level or depth of competence outlined in Chapter 2. For example, performance evidence is very bad at demonstrating knowledge and understanding and the candidate's ability to solve problems. Furthermore, providing performance evidence can be relatively resource intensive in comparison to other types of evidence and although performance evidence is crucial to determine competence, it is not crucial to provide performance evidence to cover all situations in which performance may be required. For example, in the driving test, if you can demonstrate that you can drive to the acceptable standard during the test, it is seen as acceptable that you *know* how to drive differently in wet conditions. It would not make a great deal of sense to wait until it rains to assess the driver again in those conditions (and others) when the benefits are likely to be marginal.

For this reason, evidence of knowledge or knowledge evidence is used to determine the learner's:

● knowledge of facts, (procedures, location of equipment, legislation, etc)
● understanding of principles and theories etc
● understanding of how they would adapt their performance in different situations
● understanding of how they would handle contingencies
● application of knowledge.

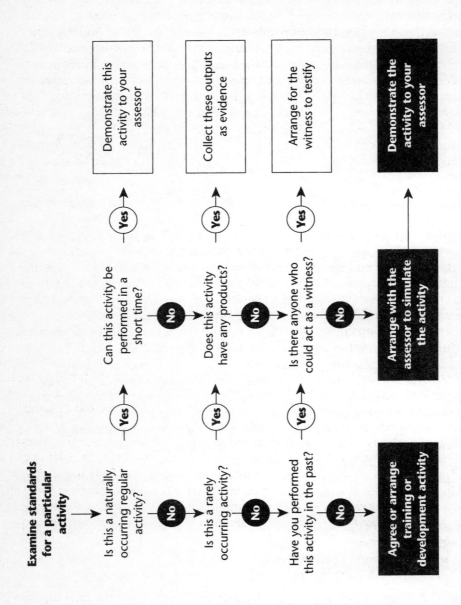

Figure 5.1 Appropriate evidence flow chart

The source of knowledge evidence is the learner. The most cost effective and appropriate way of determining whether or not the learner has the appropriate level of knowledge and understanding is through questioning by the assessor. One of the principal differences between performance evidence and knowledge evidence is that the production of good quality knowledge evidence is, to a greater degree, outside the direct control of the learner. The efficient production of good knowledge evidence is dependent upon the questioning technique and skills of the assessor.

Questioning

The assessor requires one skill above all others, the skill to question. Questioning is used in the assessment of performance to:

- confirm the questioner's understanding of the demonstrated performance
- motivate the learner
- establish the learner's level of understanding
- confirm agreement with the learner
- establish the authenticity of evidence
- encourage the learner to solve problems
- establish the learner's contingency plans
- establish a rapport
- explore the learner's opinions and ideas.

We are all familiar with questioning and as the saying goes, 'familiarity breeds contempt'. Good questioning skills are not something we are all born with, they are skills that need to be developed and exercised in order that we can retain and perfect them.

Questioning is used to determine the degree of knowledge and understanding of the learner. This is done by obtaining information from the learner, and questions need to be designed to invite the learner to provide that information. It therefore stands to reason that the questioner must have a clear understanding of the information needed in order to determine whether or not the learner has adequate knowledge and understanding.

Choosing the right question

There is a range of different types of questions that the assessor can employ to accomplish the aims listed above, there is only one that should be avoided and that is the leading question. A leading question is one whereby the answer is suggested in the question. The problem with the leading question is that, although it is usually used to try and help the learner, it never will. It is unlikely that the learner will express anything other than the response indicated in the question, whether they believe it or not. It helps no one because if the questioner wants to know what the learner believes they cannot. Even if the learner does agree with their reply, since it was a leading question, the questioner cannot be sure.

Closed questions can become leading questions if they are not used in the correct context, so should be used with care. With that one proviso, closed questions are extremely useful and are used to confirm what we already know. All assessment situations will involve some use of closed questions. Questioners may use closed questions to:

- summarize information provided by the learner
- clarify what they believe has been said or done
- confirm that the learner has understood the question.

Open questions are the most useful questions to ask learners. These questions are open-ended short questions, and begin with words such as how, who, why, what, where, and when. They allow the learner to provide the information you require, in their own words.

Probing questions or follow-up questions are usually asked after the reply to open questions, where the learner has not provided the information you required. The probing question is used to further refine the information provided by the learner. They are usually in the form of further open questions targeting some specific information which has not been forthcoming in the original answer or asking the learner to elaborate on one particular aspect of their reply.

Questioning technique

Choosing the appropriate type of question is only one aspect of questioning technique. A good questioner is a good listener. A good listener cannot listen adequately to a learner and compose their next question. That is why the questioner should always prepare their questions in advance, where this is possible. Obviously probing questions cannot usually be anticipated but the main opening questions can. Always devote all your attention to the reply of the listener and fully concentrate. This does not mean that you cannot make brief notes to trigger you memory, but those notes should be in the form of one key word wherever possible. The learner will always forgive the questioner if they need a few seconds to formulate a follow-up question, but may not forgive a questioner who does not listen.

A good questioning technique is also dependent upon a supportive and nurturing attitude. A good questioner will avoid:

- questions which may imply a criticism of the learner or other colleagues
- consecutive 'why' questions (this can be threatening, making the learner feel as if they are being interrogated)
- using questioning to demonstrate their own expertise
- being judgmental about the learner's beliefs
- becoming argumentative with the learner.

When the questioning is directly linked to an activity that is being performed by the learner, it can be enormously effective. Creating a natural discourse between the learner and their questioner will make the process less intimidating for the learner.

If the assessment is being performed as part of an NVQ assessment, it should be remembered that the questioning process needs to be recorded in some way even if it is simply a short note from the assessor outlining what the questioning covered and the result of the questioning.

JUDGING AND RECORDING EVIDENCE

The assessor's principal role is to judge the evidence presented by learners and record their judgement. The judgement of evidence requires the assessor to scrutinize the evidence and determine whether it demonstrates that the candidate can perform consistently to the standard. Assessors need to determine that the evidence:

- is valid – it shows that the learner has met the needs of the standards
- is authentic – is the work of the candidate or in the case of evidence of teamwork, the candidate's contribution is determined.

After determining the validity and authenticity of the evidence, the assessor needs to determine if the evidence is sufficient to agree that the competence has been achieved consistently over a period of time.

If the assessment is for the purposes of an NVQ, the evidence must:

- cover all the performance criteria
- meet all the evidence requirements
- cover all the range statements
- demonstrate that the learner has all the specified knowledge and understanding
- demonstrate that the learner's competence is current at the time of assessment.

The method of recording the judgement will be determined to some degree by the reason for the assessment. If the assessment is part of a selection process or a training needs analysis, it may not require the same level of documentation as it may for a national qualification which will need to be verified by others at a later stage.

An NVQ assessment requires clear and accurate recording mechanisms so as to aid the understanding of verifiers who will confirm the assessment decisions. Although this may be a level of quality assurance that would not be required of the learning organization, it is best practice. Since it is designed to be seen by people other than the assessor and the learner it needs to be clear exactly how the assessor arrived at her decision. The actual construction and format of the recording mechanism should clearly:

- identify the assessor and the learner
- identify the standard that has been achieved
- describe the nature of evidence that was used to make that decision
- identify the location of that evidence
- state the date and venue of assessment activities
- state the date on which the learner was deemed competent.

The actual document in which these details would be recorded could be the appraisal documents, the learner's training and development plan, the organization's selection documentation and not necessarily an NVQ recording system.

6

MANAGING QUALITY, MANAGING CHANGE

Summary
In this chapter you will learn about:
• how learning organizations can use quality as a focus for their learning
• how managers can encourage a quality culture
• some of the techniques for problem-solving and developing quality initiatives
• how experimentation is crucial to the learning organization

A learning organization needs to be able to evaluate and develop new solutions to problems. If, as mentioned earlier, learning is about changing behaviour, then the manager in a learning organization is managing change. Yet a learning organization does not change for the sake of change itself, so why then does a learning organization change? It could change to adapt its products or services to new markets, to differentiate its products or services from its competitors, to increase productivity or efficiency, in short to create a competitive advantage. All organizations have personnel and all personnel think. Some of those personnel will have ideas that could help create this competitive advantage. One of the differences between a learning organization and others is that a learning organization is able to harness the intellect of all its workforce to improve quality and to help create a competitive advantage.

HARNESSING THE INTELLECT OF THE WORK-FORCE

In many organizations making a suggestion that could be beneficial to the organization could have a detrimental effect on the individual making the suggestion. For example, if you discovered that a job involving yourself and four others could be done by one person if certain equipment was modified, would you be inclined to make the suggestion and be responsible for four friends and colleagues (maybe even yourself) being made redundant? Would you question your manager's new method of working when you knew that another method would be far more effective, if it was clear that she had staked her reputation on it working, and she would be responsible for your salary review?

The learning organization manages to encourage suggestions and the questioning of working practices by ensuring that the individual is rewarded not punished for their contribution. Some learning organizations do this by a contract with their workforce that as far as possible, guarantees the jobs of the work-force. Therefore, initiatives which lead to job displacement do not lead to redundancies. Some may provide financial and other rewards for suggestions, but none of these measures are particularly effective unless the culture of the organization encourages and nurtures a creative and questioning approach among its work-force.

The learning organization is proactive and influences what happens in its organization. Simply providing an atmosphere where suggestions are welcomed is a reactive response and is only part of the learning organization's response.

The manager's role

The manager in a learning organization is in a pivotal role for the organization. It is the manager who encourages quality enhancement in many ways, as she can:

- provide the main channel of communication for the organization, spreading enthusiasm for the need to find new and better ways of working and better quality products or services
- empower staff to make changes in working practices where this will improve quality
- act as a conduit for promoting and publicizing the ideas brought forward by members of her team
- encourage and promote work and initiatives which will cross different organizational or departmental boundaries
- act as a facilitator with her subordinates to solve problems and improve quality.

A manager that only pays lip service to a quality development programme will do untold damage by demoralizing rather than energizing their team. However, implementing a quality programme can engender self-respect and self-esteem in employees because it is recognizing that they are the experts in their area and that the organization's management values their thoughts and opinions.

Communicating quality

The attitude of the work-force is crucial to a successful quality programme and the attitude of the work-force is itself dependent upon the attitude of the management. A top level commitment to a quality programme should be evident to all employees. A quality improvement policy which flows from this commitment needs to be communicated to the work-force, not once, but in all the things that managers say and do.

Often managers believe that communication is about what they say, however this covers only a fraction of what communication is about. We communicate messages to each other in the way we dress, the way we act, react, what we ignore as well as what we pay attention to, what we do and what we don't do. Managers will not communicate effectively if they plead with subordinates that they need to pursue a quality improvement programme while they do not assign appropriate resources and attention to helping the quality programme succeed, or they don't actively support staff who are implementing quality initiatives. The decisive factor in the communication of ideas is never what is said or even thought – it is what is done. Managers in an effective learning organization are leaders, they will demonstrate behaviour which supports and encourages the learning of others but most of all they will learn themselves.

Empowering staff to improve quality

Wherever possible, staff should be empowered to make changes to their own job role where this could improve performance. Staff should be clearly allocated areas of activity where the success of those functions is their responsibility. If those staff wish to make changes to the way that they work in order to improve quality or productivity, they should have the freedom to do so. Naturally this needs to be done within a management framework which not only allows and encourages such experimentation but also evaluates the effectiveness of those changes. All staff should be given the power to innovate. Where the resources required to implement the new initiative go beyond those already allocated, the management should seriously consider a proposal for increased resources. Where, for good budgetary or strategic reasons, innovative suggestions are not to be implemented, the innovators should receive complete and full feedback regarding the reasons for not implementing their ideas.

Championing quality initiatives

The manager's role extends beyond her immediate team or area of responsibility. In a learning organization it is important that maximum use is made of all learning that occurs. This will mean that where lessons are learned by the manager's team, that learning is broadcast to others who may benefit in different areas of the organization. This will have three main effects and will encourage others to:

- implement the new initiative
- further develop or adapt the initiative
- find their own solutions to their problems.

Variety in teams

A key ingredient of learning organizations is that of variety, be it variety in strategies, in systems, in structures, but most of all in teams. Group learning is stimulated by different responses to the paradoxes and contradictions which arise within the operation of the organization. People with different skills and ways of working from different backgrounds, when harnessed cooperatively towards achieving a common goal, will be far more creative than a team of like-minded individuals.

Further variety can be introduced by encouraging interdepartmental or interteam activities as such interaction across departmental boundaries will assist learning. The manager can be proactive in this respect, thereby exposing the team's systems and procedures to the scrutiny and questioning of different perspectives. It should also help to further develop the team who can improve their understanding of the work undertaken in other sections of the organization. This interaction could and should extend to social as well as operational contacts.

Problem solving

Although the manager should not be seen as the team's problem-solver, she should be active in developing solutions to business problems. The team should be responsible for finding solutions which will help to develop a competitive advantage for the organization. The manager's role in problem-solving can be to use problem-solving tools to provoke and stimulate creative thought about the organization's problems.

In order to facilitate the best response from other team members to the problem solving process, it is important that the manager adopts a participative leadership style. This way, team members will be encouraged to participate, their views will always be sought and valued. It should be remembered that each problem is a new challenge. The contribution of each team member in the past is no indication of who will provide the creative spark that will solve this new problem. The team can and should be used to generate solutions not simply to be a method of validating solutions, proposed by the manager.

QUALITY

The first lesson for all learning organizations is that to learn, to create a competitive advantage the whole organization needs to focus on quality. The quality of the product or service produced and the quality of the way the organization produces their output or delivers their service.

Often the word quality is mistakenly read as 'higher quality' or 'luxury' when in fact it simply means meeting the customer requirements or in other words being *fit for its intended purpose*.

Ralph Barra (1989) identifies ten 'quality enhancement conditions' which can be used by an organization to assess what how far they will need to go towards improving quality. The checklist in Table 6.1 builds upon those ten conditions to produce a checklist which can help organizations to identify actions they need to establish in order that quality enhancement is encouraged and supported.

These questions simply outline the areas that an organization needs to examine in order that quality is addressed. Each organization will need to define their own specific quality conditions and establish their own quality programme.

Having a quality plan and encouraging the work-force to participate in the delivery of that plan is the first important step on the road to a quality assured organization.

Quality management

The manager's primary role in a learning organization is to coach and develop staff. The manager is there to help staff to achieve their potential within the job role. Managers in learning organizations realize that the work-force are their main resource, it is they who will provide the new ideas, it is they who will provide key sources of new initiatives. When it comes to implementing a quality plan the contribution and commitment of all staff is crucial to its success.

Quality circles

Quality circles are a way of enabling people to contribute to improving their jobs, thus enabling the employee to critically engage with the job of work they are performing. It provides a structured way for employees to become actively involved in cooperative problem-solving. Quality

Table 6.1 The 'ten quality enhancement conditions'

Question	Yes	No	Action

Strategic plan
Does the organization's business or strategic plan incorporate quality issues? Does it include SMART (Specific, Measurable, Achievable, Realistic and Time-bound) targets for the development of quality in the organization? Is the quality of the organization's products or services enshrined in the strategic plan? Is the further development of that quality identified as one of the pre-eminent goals of the organization?

Quality programme plan
Do you have one?
Is it geared to prevent poor quality?

Customer's perception
Do you know what your customer expects?
Do you respond to those expectations?
Do you have mechanisms which will identify changes in customer expectations?

Design assurance
Does your research and development team design products and services to meet customer expectations?

Purchased materials
Do you assess the performance of your suppliers?
Do they meet standards for the quality of the materials supplied?
Can other suppliers provide more consistent quality?

Participative management
Does the organization's management empower staff to make changes?
Does the management support and encourage quality initiatives?

Training
Is training and development designed to facilitate quality enhancement?
Do the development and training activities of the organization contribute to improving the competence of its staff?

Advanced technology
Is there a mechanism for identifying and evaluating new and innovative procedures, processes and equipment for use by the organization?
Is it effective?
Is advanced technology implemented where appropriate?

Performance measurement
Is performance measurement accurate?
Does it identify all quality related costs?
Does it demonstrate performance trends over time?
Does it identify areas where there could be improvements?

Recognition
Is the contribution of staff to the quality programme rewarded in an appropriate way?

circles began in a few companies in Japan in the 1960s but now the concept and the philosophy has spread around the globe. As Ralph Barra explains:

> When employees are asked what to do instead of being told what to do, they respond to the challenge with more than good ideas. Morale goes up, and with it, the team spirit that motivates employees to be more productive. Employees take pride in their work. They develop a personal stake in productivity, product quality, and reliability. They welcome advanced technology because they feel they are in charge of it; there is less resistance to change because they help to initiate it. Communication between management and employees improves dramatically, and employees come to understand the role they play in their organization. These intangible benefits will often outweigh the value of the ideas themselves. (Barra, 1989, p.65)

Voluntary

One of the central tenets of quality circles is voluntariness. Quality circles must be free from coercion of any sort, something very difficult in a world where very little could be said to be truly voluntary. This ensures that the circle will have the commitment of those involved. It also means that if individuals have chosen to use their own skills and abilities to solve their work problems rather than blame others, they have also agreed to work with and have respect for people who are perhaps doing different jobs. In this way they can all work together, and all benefit from a jointly earned success.

Ownership

Since the whole concept of quality circles rests upon the assumption that participation is voluntary, it comes as no surprise to find that the participants feel a sense of ownership to the circle and to the solutions produced by the circle. The sense of ownership and commitment to the circle will only continue as long as the circle itself has ownership of its direction. The circle must decide what problems it wishes to tackle, how those problems will be tackled and their preferred solution. If circles are simply seen as a way that the work-force finds solutions to management's problems, then they will not survive simply because the commitment to a quality circle stems from the circle's ownership, not of the process but of the problem.

Management's role

To support and encourage quality circles management needs to invest them with the resources to implement change and the power to act on their decisions. The manager's role is to support the work of the quality circle and praise its successes. Managers need to provide the accommodation and all other reasonable facilities to allow the circle to meet. Yet most of all, managers need to believe that participative problem-solving is a good way of achieving the organization's goals, implementing where they can the recommendations of the circle and providing a full explanation where it is not possible to do so.

TECHNIQUES FOR IDENTIFYING AND RESOLVING QUALITY PROBLEMS

There are a number of techniques that can be employed by the manager to examine issues around quality and performance. The key issues for the manager are the identification of problems, the analysis and presentation of the problem and the production of ideas towards a solution. The techniques cannot guarantee the solving of the problem but should result in the production of a number of ideas which could lead to a solution.

Decisions based on data

A learning organization bases its decisions on empirical data where that is available, or else it will attempt to establish evidence for the decision. There is nothing wrong with managers having hunches about what can be done to improve the situation but the decision for action should be based upon empirical data. Collection of easily observable data is often all that is needed, for example, if there is a problem on one production line which is often stopped through different problems. Simply by recording the stoppage, the reason for the stoppage and the down time due to the stoppage over a reasonable period of time, should provide enough evidence to identify the main problem and hence suggest possible solutions.

Sorting, selecting and presenting data

It may be that the data collected is empirical data collected through observation. It may be sales figures, returns figures or production figures. The way this data is collected could be crucial to identifying possible problems. For this reason it is important to try to identify the different influences on the figures and produce data that can be manipulated in many different ways. This in effect means that the data must be able to be broken down into groups which are comparable. For instance, if there are two plants which are roughly similar in terms of staff and resources but one plant produces far more than another, we may want to examine other differences within the plant and compare them one against another. Through comparing different groups we may find that it is one particular team that is far better or worse than others. There is no real secret to identifying potential problems or potential improvements. It is simply a case of comparing one with another, seeing what is working well and identifying the difference in working practices, worker competence, motivation, resources that provides a better quality of product. It is only possible to do this if a very clear and concise description of the desired quality of the product has been determined. After all, the object of the operation is to provide a quality product, or to be more precise, the required amount of the product, which meets all the *required functions* to the *required quality* at the *required time,* at the lowest cost. If the product meets more than the required functions, to a higher quality and before the required time, there may be no complaints from customers, and no returns but clearly extra costs have been built into the product production. This will certainly mean that there is scope for reducing costs. It could be that the definition of the product is changed to reflect the higher quality and the product is repositioned within the market-place to attract a higher price but this in itself could have far reaching financial implications.

LEADING DISCUSSIONS

One of the manager's roles in a learning organization is to assist with the problem solving or quality improvement process. One of the most efficient ways of contributing to this process is to facilitate group working and discussion. The natural position for the manager in a learning organization is as a lead and guide to the discussion. As the leader of the discussion, the manager is responsible for helping all the other members of the group to think through a particular aspect of work, she is not there to brief or teach the group. Through leading the discussion the manager may ask questions to clarify what has been said, and challenge assumptions, but this should be done in an open and non-threatening, non-critical manner. Although discussions of this sort may not identify solutions every time, they should develop a shared understanding of the problem or topic.

In leading discussions, the manager should have a clear view of what the objective of the discussion, even if the objective is to arrive at a common understanding of the job.

Examine the subject

It is often useful if the manager has had an opportunity to examine the topic in terms of a logical sequence which can then be broken down and analysed in greater depth by the group. When determining the disaggregation of the topic or problem, the manager should look at the amount of time that is available for the discussion and try to assess what can be achieved in the time available.

A common problem when assessing topics for discussion is that our natural proclivity for reductionism that has been carefully honed by schools, colleges and universities, can isolate the subject from its context. It can encourage us to seek solutions to what appears a small problem without examining its impact on the remainder of the process or the organization. Therefore, it is important to place the topic in relation to the rest of the organization and how any changes may effect others.

If the discussion has value it is worth recording. A common method for leading discussions is by using flip-charts to help record and structure the discussion. This will allow the manager to prepare headings for discussion and record the views of the group as they happen.

Introducing the topic

The introduction of the discussion is important as it will place the discussion in a context. It should outline:

- why it is important to address the topic
- why it is important to address it at this time
- a common understanding of the issues involved.

The introduction should arouse the interest of the group and provide clear objectives for the discussion. The outline of the topic and even the objectives of the discussion may need to be refined on the basis of contributions from the group.

Leading the discussion

The manager has a number of objectives when leading a discussion, she is trying to:

- ensure the maximum participation of all members of the group
- listen to and understand all the contributions
- ensure that other members of the group understand the contributions

- accurately summarize and record contributions
- meet the objectives of the discussion
- keep contributions relevant to the topic under discussion
- clarify areas of confusion
- conclude the discussion in the time allowed.

The three main tools in the armoury of the manager to assist her in meeting these objectives are questioning, silence and summaries.

Questioning has been covered in some detail as part of the previous chapter and there are only a few things to add here. The quality of the discussion will be determined to a great degree by the questioning skills of the manager. Open questions should be used to provoke thought and open up discussion, closed questions paraphrasing what has been said should be used to clarify the group and the manager's understanding. Direct questions should also be used to encourage members of the group to contribute ('what do you think, John?'). As well as these types of questions, general statements and assumptions should be tested out by asking for specific examples to illustrate points. Often it is more valuable to the discussion if the manager can determine *why* members of the group believe something rather than simply ascertaining what they believe. It should not be forgotten that the success of the discussion is predicated upon the willing participation of the members of the group. Therefore any questioning that could be seen as threatening, point scoring, or which could lead to the embarrassment of members of the group could result in the withdrawal of participation from one or all of the group.

Silence is a powerful tool that can be employed by the manager. When there is a silence in response to a question, an unseen pressure builds within the group at the uneasiness or embarrassment created by the silence. Each member of the group feels the pressure and this can assist in moving the discussion on. This does not mean that the manager is immune to this pressure to break the silence, indeed it could be argued that they feel the pressure even more intensely because of their responsibility for the group. Yet as long as the manager is satisfied that the group has understood the question it is important that the manager does not give in to the temptation to break the silence. Silences can be useful thinking points within the discussion, times where questions can be thought through.

Summaries are used by the manager to pull together the disparate contributions and record them. Summaries will generally paraphrase what has already been said and express the consensus achieved. They should be agreed with the group as an accurate reflection of the discussion and also draw the discussions into a coherent whole.

Pitfalls to avoid

There are a few possible problems which could hinder the proper operation of a discussion group, but all can be easily dealt with by a competent manager using questioning, and summarizing.

Silence

It should not be assumed that silence means acceptance of what has been said. Silence from members of the group could mean that they:

- have not heard
- have not understood
- are shy.

If members of the group are silent it is up to the manager to encourage them to contribute from their experience. If the individual is indeed shy then the manager will need to encourage the contribution without drawing too much attention to them.

Specialists/seniors

The presence of specialists or more senior staff in the group could lead to members of the group deferring to the views of these people and not making their own contribution. It is important that the manager demonstrates that all contributions are required and that all the group need to fully understand the topic under discussion.

Monopoly players

There may be a particular individual or individuals who are monopolizing the discussion. The manager, although welcoming the contributions, needs to still make spaces for the contributions of others without offending the talkative individual.

Evaluation

To help a leader of a meeting to assess their own performance in the meeting they may find it helpful to use a checklist similar to the one in Table 6.2. This simple checklist was derived from the MCI element D2.1 Lead meetings. Here, questions on the list correspond to the performance criteria from the element. Although it is somewhat simpler and includes questions over and above what is required by the element, it is easy to see that an individual who was to achieve the D2.1 element would consistently answer yes to all the questions. The same questions could be used

Table 6.2 Leading discussions and meetings: an evaluations checklist

Leading discussions and meetings: an evaluation checklist	Yes	No
Did you provide sufficient notice of the meeting?		
Did everyone agree the objectives of the meeting?		
Was the time allocated to the discussion appropriate and adequate?		
Did you actively encourage contributions from all members?		
Did you keep the discussion focused on the topic?		
Did your interventions aid the understanding of the topic?		
Were conflicting views explored?		
Did you clearly and accurately summarize at appropriate points?		
Did the meeting achieve its objectives?		
Did agreed recommendations or decisions fall within the authority of the group?		
Did you communicate the decisions or recommendations of the group to those who need it?		
Did you seek feedback from the group as to your effectiveness in leading the discussion?		

with some very minor modifications by an assessor who was to observe a candidate performing in a meeting or leading a discussion.

BRAINSTORMING

This technique is used to generate a large number of ideas. The technique should help people to think laterally as they adapt and expand on other ideas produced by the group. Brainstorming is often a useful way to identify possible problems or causes of known problems but can be used to generate ideas on any subject.

The ideas are created because all members of the group are involved and encouraged to participate and all suggestions are recorded without any comments or criticism. Although there are a number of variations as to how people prefer to run brainstorming sessions it is usually most productive if each member of the group contributes in turn (however, people should be allowed to pass if they feel that they cannot contribute). Only when all the members of the group have exhausted their ideas should the session finish.

The group is then left with a large number of ideas which need further analysis in order that they can be properly interpreted and assessed. There are a number of structured brainstorming techniques which will help to focus the ideas of the group especially the *cause and effect diagram,* the *why–why diagram* and the *how–how diagram.*

Cause and effect diagram

Sometimes known as a fishbone diagram, this is a simple way to categorize the ideas from a brainstorming session, where those ideas are possible causes for a particular effect. This can help the group to visualize the problem, refine the suggestions, identify further ideas or even eliminate some.

How it works

The effect or problem is written in a box on the right hand side of a flipchart. The possible causes (anything that may result in the effect) are then grouped together and linked to the effect. Each of these groupings is given a label which can then help to focus the group to discover other possible causes. This method can be used to categorize suggestions produced from a brainstorm or to focus a brainstorming session around a particular problem. The resultant shape of the diagram explains the fishbone name used to describe it (see Figure 6.1).

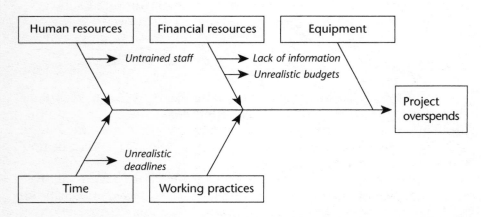

Figure 6.1 Example of a cause and effect diagram

Why–why and how–how diagrams

A why–why diagram is used to identify all the possible causes of a particular problem. In many ways the how–how diagram is the reverse of the why–why diagram. In the why–why diagram the problem is written onto a flipchart and the group is asked to answer the question 'why'? All the suggested answers are recorded. Then for each of these answers in turn, the group is again asked 'why'? This is repeated until the group feels that it cannot usefully continue any further. As the results are recorded a detailed picture of possible causes is produced (see Figure 6.2).

In the how–how diagram, the process is the same but instead of examining the problem the how–how diagram looks to discover all the possible solutions. The how–how diagram takes a general statement of a solution and asks the question 'how'? of each answer. The how–how and why–why type of analysis are good ways of ensuring that the group looks at all the possible solutions or all the possible causes rather than focusing on the most obvious.

SORTING AND SELECTING

Producing large numbers of ideas is the first stage. The second task of the group is to make judgements on the ideas produced. Although using consensus to select the problems or solutions to pursue will not guarantee the correct result every time, its probably the safest and most comfortable way to start. At least that way, if it turns out to be wrong, you are not alone. There are many ways of selecting and ranking the ideas produced through brainstorming. One way would be to ask each member of the group to allocate a ranking (maybe the top three) to the list of ideas, followed by the group leader adding up the scores and determining the selection. Another way would be to write the ideas on cards and allow the group to discuss the relative positions of each idea. This can be especially useful in encouraging the group to discuss the relative merits of different solutions and comparing one with another.

EXPERIMENTING AND TAKING RISKS

Experimenting or risk-taking is crucial to the successful learning organization. Success will mean rewards for the organization and failure will mean costs. A learning organization should benefit from both success and failure because even in failure, the learning organization should be able to learn lessons which will enable it to secure a higher ratio of successes in the future.

On one level, experimentation is simply empowering and encouraging people to use their own initiative. Or in other words, learning from past experiences and making a change to their usual behaviour because they believe that the change will be advantageous. The manager in a learning organization is in a pivotal position to make experimentation and the use of initiative part of the organization's culture.

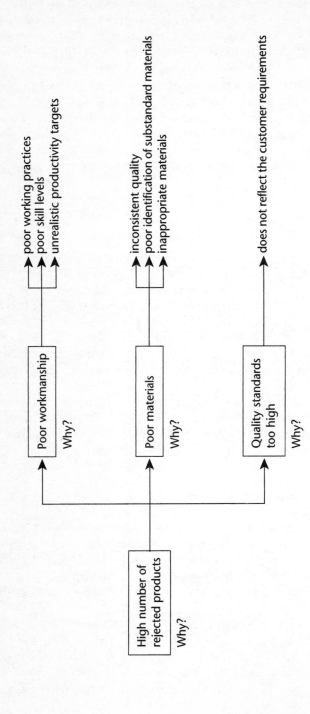

Figure 6.2 Example of a why–why diagram

This seems such a straightforward and simple piece of 'common sense' but we all have had experiences of people who have slavishly followed procedures and actions which are clearly inappropriate to the situation. Terrible disasters often involve people following orders or procedures without either taking account of changing circumstances or else, not feeling sufficiently confident to act outside those procedures and hence incurring the wrath of their superiors.

Barriers to using initiative

Why do people refrain from changing their behaviour to fit the circumstance? There are a number of reasons:

- they do not believe they are *allowed* to change from the specified routine
- they told their manager that the procedures would never work and this (problem) will only serve to prove the point
- they will lose face if they make a change
- they believe that failure, after acting on their initiative, will be punished
- they are not sure that the solution would be successful.

People are rarely punished for not taking risks. Yet, if the culture of the organization leads to no one taking risks, innovation would cease and the organization would decline. The manager can create the climate where risk-taking and innovation are commonplace. The way to achieve this is through minimising the risks, rewarding successful risk taking and in the process, developing a positive attitude towards experimentation within the organization.

Minimizing the risk

There are a number of ways to ensure that the risk to the organization is minimized:

1. *Assess the risk,* assess the maximum cost to the organization if the action is judged to be unsuccessful. Assess the maximum benefit to the organization if the action is successful. Discuss the action with others and establish if similar action was pursued in the past, and see what can be learned from those experiences. Discuss with others the action or risk that you intend to take, find out if they agree with your assessment of the possible costs and benefits and seek their advice.
2. *Make a decision,* this should only be done after assessing the risk. Risk taking is only done to achieve a goal, and only because all safe

established routes have been exhausted. Risk-taking is never done for the sake of it, there must be tangible benefits to the organization from the success of the activity. If the worst case scenario is something that could be coped with, and it is still felt that the risk is worth taking, then the decision must be to go ahead with the activity.

3. *Plan the action,* think through the entire activity, the effects of the activity on different sections of the organization and carefully plan each step. Think through the possibility of failure and try to identify early indicators of failure. Develop a contingency plan and determine the stage at which it would need to be implemented.

4. *Act with confidence,* when the decision has been made to act, make sure that the action is taken with confidence. It is vital that the action is taken with the belief that it will succeed.

5. *Review and learn from the experiment*, all experiments will provide a learning opportunity. In a learning organization the success or failure of the initiative needs to be properly analysed and then communicated to others in the organization who may benefit. It could be that the experiment was successful, partially successful, or a failure. Whatever the outcome it is important that the lessons are learned and recorded so that they may be used to form the basis of further experimentation.

Encouraging the culture

The manager can help to facilitate the risk-taking and experimenting culture by:

- praising individuals who are prepared to take risks
- rewards such as salaries, bonuses and promotion are designed to encourage risk-taking
- failure in itself is not punished, (ie, the budgets are not cut, the individual does not lose salary or other rewards)
- people are encouraged to discuss ideas throughout the organization
- resources for experimenting are made available
- everyone is allowed an input into the decision-making process
- when things go wrong individuals are supported and encouraged to learn from their mistakes
- taking risks and experimenting with procedures and systems form part of job descriptions and job specifications.

PART 2: DEVELOPING PEOPLE

There is only one asset that an organization has that can appreciate in value: the human resource. Properly developed, the human resource can transform even the most productive of organizations. A sustainable learning or development programme for an organization rests upon the flexibility of the learning activities. The way in which learning takes place has to meet the needs of the learners and the organization but it must also be effective at developing competence. Part 2 will look at some of the most effective and efficient ways in which an employer can develop staff without resorting to 'training courses.' It will look at how the organization can support learning and how the individual's learning can contribute towards the organization's learning.

7

LEARNING AND COACHING

```
┌─────────────────────────────────────────────────────────────────┐
```

Summary

This chapter will look at:

- learning theory and how that theory can be put into the practical application of coaching

- motivation

- coaching, what it is and how a coaching culture can be encouraged.

```
└─────────────────────────────────────────────────────────────────┘
```

LEARNING THEORY

Theories of how people learn have occupied psychologists and educationalists for many years. A simple classification or categorization of learning theory would divide between *cognitive* and *connectionist* models.

Cognitive models of learning look at the perceptions, insights and attitudes (or cognitions) people have about themselves and their environment. For cognitive theorists, learning is the way these cognitions are modified by experience. Often learning occurs suddenly, we suddenly come to the realization that we now really understand. This is explained by cognitive theory as the modification of the learner's cognition, the whole situation is now seen in a new way by the learner. It is believed that this type of learning is particularly valuable as it is not easily forgotten and can be easily adapted to new situations.

Connectionist models assume that all responses are invoked by a particular stimulus. For the connectionist, all learning is the way in which the affinity between a stimulus and the response changes with experience. These stimuli can be positive and negative, a carrot and a stick, some stimuli may encourage a particular behaviour and others may inhibit a particular behaviour.

These are of course polemical positions and the main-stream position is as usual, different combinations of elements from both theories. It is important to recognize the key concepts of connectionist and cognitive learning theory to help gain an understanding of just how an individual learns and consequently, how you can contribute to and encourage learning.

The role of actively assisting in an individual's development is to create the circumstances in which learning can take place, providing for the learner:

- the opportunities to practise skills,
- an example of competent performance
- a source of information and advice
- feedback on their performance
- a guide to direct them towards new insights and understanding.

Often learning is done in a classroom, school or other educational environment. However, when the behaviour that needs to be learnt is an occupational skill or ability, it is often easier to create the circumstances which will encourage learning through coaching or experiential learning.

The main benefit of learning through real working experiences, guided by a colleague or mentor is that the techniques employed lead to meaningful learning as opposed to the rote learning process many of us experienced at school.

Learning through real work experiences means that the learner has been placed in a position of trust and responsibility, they have a chance to practise in a real situation with supervision and any mistakes can be capitalized on through reflection with their manager, trainer or mentor. However, most important of all, the experience is *owned* by the learner.

This way of learning treats the learner with dignity and respect, itself inherently motivating, but more than that, it provides lasting lessons for the learner, creating experiences which will live on long past the time where the learner becomes competent.

MOTIVATION

The key to successful learning is motivation. It is the energy that drives forward a learning organization and its significance should never be underestimated. Indeed, the structure of a learning organization is designed to promote a motivated work-force.

Learners are naturally self-motivated and can manage their own learning for tasks that they see as interesting, fun, meaningful, or relevant in some way. Usually, this will mean any activities that either meet personal goals, encourage a feeling of well-being or encourage respect from their peers. Yet motivation may be lacking when individuals are asked to learn something:

- that does not particularly interest them
- they have little or no control or choice over
- they lack adequate support, respect and encouragement for.

To enhance motivation to learn, we need to excite the learner and ensure control and choice is open to the learner.

In many formal learning situations choices are limited. Yet, when personal development is not restricted to such formal learning and prescribed syllabi, the opportunities for learners to determine their own goals and control their own learning processes is much greater. To encourage and motivate the learner, they will need to view the learning experience as meaningful, and not simply an activity determined and controlled by them.

It is important to remember that motivation comes from within the learner, all we can do is provide the types of learning opportunities and support for the learner to nourish that motivation. A motivated learner will be conscious of the learning process and their position within it, they will evaluate the relevance of each learning opportunity for themselves, and understand their own strengths and weaknesses.

To support motivation we should provide learning opportunities which:

- *Will be seen as relevant to the needs of the learner*. This means that it is important that the learner is involved in identifying her own learning needs and takes ownership of those needs. It may be that the organization has changed the ways in which it operates which has created the learning gap. In such circumstances, it is important that the learner fully recognizes the need for the operational change before they can accept the need for their own learning. It does not matter how clear that it may be to anyone else that this individual has a training need if that individual does not.
- *Challenge the learner, often presenting them with added responsibilities*. If a learning opportunity is to be effective it must stretch the individual. This has two main consequences, it demonstrates to the learner that you have confidence in them and it ends with a real sense of achievement. Although, in such situations, learners should be monitored and supported, the responsibility for completing the task should be theirs. The successful completion of a learning task which challenges the learner will build their confidence. Alternatively, if the task is beyond the learner, failure can dent their confidence. Consequently, it is important that activities are chosen which are achievable, and the learner is closely monitored and supported.

- *Provide choice and hence a level of control over how, where and when to engage in the activity.* Just as it is important for the learner to be involved in determining their own learning needs, they also need to see how the learning activity will contribute to new levels of skill and understanding. Not only do learners have an important perspective on their own learning, they are more likely to work harder and persevere with an activity that they have a sense of ownership for.
- *Will engender respect from their peers.* The learning activity should have value in itself, and it should be generally perceived as valuable. This will mean that the achievement of the learning activity itself will generate respect from colleagues and friends.
- *Are fun.* Wherever possible, find out what the learner enjoys doing. Does she have a hobby, a pastime or an interest which could provide an angle to make the activity more enjoyable?

If we can provide learning opportunities which do all this, and we provide the support and guidance to enable the learner to gain maximum benefit from the learning opportunity, motivation will not be a problem.

WHAT IS COACHING?

The vast majority of us learn at work. Recent surveys have shown that the main method of training is through on-the-job coaching. It is extremely effective, tailored to the individual learner, designed to fulfil the needs of the organization and is cost efficient to boot. However, it is usually done informally with little or no support for the individual passing on their skills – often they are not aware they are doing it. The main reason for this is the prevalence of two erroneous assumptions. First, coaching people in a one-to-one relationship is seen as natural and easy when it is neither. Second, it is assumed that all a coach requires is the technical skills and knowledge to perform the given task. These two assumptions lead to a lack of support, training and development and the undervaluing of the coaching role.

Yet coaching enables skills and experience to be passed from one employee to another in a way that is cost effective because it minimizes disruption to the work-place (see Table 7.1). Consequently, organizations are increasingly recognizing the need to develop the skills of their work-force through regular coaching rather than traditional courses and events.

To be a coach, an individual needs a number of skills. As in any other area of life, some people will find it easier to develop those skills than others. The coach requires the technical skills and knowledge of the activity she is to coach *and* coaching skills. The skills of a coach are many and varied and can include the ability to:

Table 7.1 The benefits of coaching

	Coaching	Off-the-job training
Time	Coaching will prove to take up a fraction of the time as it is integrated into the learner's working activities. Any activities which would fall outside the learner's normal work role could be planned to coincide with periods of seasonal or demand related inactivity.	Training will usually be fitted into a set time-scale, determined by the training provider/college. The time-scale is unlikely to take into account the needs of the organization. The overall length of time is likely to be much greater than that of the coached learner.
Flexibility	The development can be structured around the needs of the learner, her learning style, her job and the organization.	The training will be structured around the needs of the training provider and all the learners on the course. It is very difficult (but not impossible) to address the learning styles of all learners on the course.
Cost	The cash costs are a fraction of those for off-the-job training. However, there is significant cost involved in the training, development and support of coaches. There will also be some cost incurred with time spent off-the-job by coaches.	Usually much more expensive than coaching in cash terms. Yet, the overall cost is cheaper because there is no resource cost for other members of the organization.
Organization	The preparation, organization and evaluation of the learner's development will take time and effort on the part of the coach.	All preparation, organization and evaluation of the learner's development is taken care of by the training provider.
Productivity	The learner remains productive during the learning process and should achieve maximum productivity quicker.	The learner is not usually productive to the organization during the training.
Quality	The development is more likely to meet the needs of the learner and the organization. The learning should cover specific job-related issues and skills as well as the organizational procedures and requirements. The learner is learning from someone who is currently performing the activity.	The training is less likely to meet the specific needs of the learner or the organization. The training is likely to be more generic focusing on general issues and procedures. The learner will need to interpret the learning in terms of her specific job. Often, needing further job or organization-specific training to supplement her off-the-job training.

- assess skills and knowledge
- identify learning opportunities
- plan and structure learning opportunities
- evaluate learning opportunities
- organize and manage their time
- actively listen
- identify learning styles
- motivate learners
- demonstrate skills and abilities
- articulate technical knowledge in a way that the learner will understand.

WHAT DOES A COACH DO?

Coaching is the passing on of the skills and experience of one employee to another, in a way that is non-disruptive to the organization. The role of the coach is to identify with the learner, the gaps in their learning and plan appropriate learning experiences to meet those needs. Ideally, all those with a supervisory or management role should be required to act as a coach in a learning organization. The coach's role is to work with the learner to identify their development needs and using their own experience and competence in those areas as a basis to provide learning opportunities. The coach will also monitor, motivate and support the learner to achieve those goals.

The learning opportunities provided for the learner fall into two main categories: (1) carefully chosen work activities which will become progressively more demanding and, where appropriate, (2) demonstrations from the coach.

Providing opportunities and experiences

The skill of the coach is to provide genuinely challenging activities for the learner while at the same time ensuring that it falls within the ability of the learner. The coach should seek to provide opportunities which contribute to the overall development plan of the learner. For example, if the learner has a learning need for project management skills, it would be sensible to provide opportunities where the learner could become progressively involved in the running of projects.

Coaching is especially useful in developing additional skills, perhaps to prepare learners for promotion, or for elements of a qualification. These work activities or learning opportunities should arise where possible from the job role, but many will spring from special tasks or job swaps. No matter where the source of the learning opportunity, it should always be a 'real' situation. This means that after preparing the learner for the task the coach should take a back seat, letting the learner make the decisions and manage the task. This way, the benefits of the learning experience are multiplied because the learner proves to herself as well as to others that she can accomplish the task without help. It is important that there is an opportunity for the learner to fail in order for the learning opportunity to be 'real'.

However, the coach should ensure that wherever possible the learner will not fail. One way to achieve this is to ensure that the learner is quite clear about her responsibility for the learning activity, and is fully prepared for the task. This can only be achieved through detailed and careful briefing from the coach. It is important that the learner is involved in agreeing her learning needs but the tasks must be selected because the coach believes that they can be achieved. However, this is not something to be broadcast to others. It is enough to say that the learner is undertaking this activity because the coach wishes them to do it and the coach is confident that they can successfully achieve it.

Wherever possible mistakes should be avoided. However, mistakes are a fact of life and will occur. The learning organization recognizes that mistakes cannot be totally eradicated and if the organization does not learn from them, the same mistakes will continue to be made. If the learner does make mistakes, it is important that they learn from them. This can only be done in an organizational culture where mistakes are identified and put right at the earliest opportunity, where mistakes are not punished and where the correction of, and learning from errors, is valued and encouraged.

Ten rules for coaches

1. Never blame a learner for mistakes in a coaching situation.
2. Ensure that all coaching tasks are challenging.
3. Appraise all learning with the learner.
4. Help the learner to think for themselves.
5. Do not solve the learner's problems for them.
6. Never argue with the learner.
7. Emphasize that the development of staff is the key role of *all* managers.
8. Encourage the learner to make their own decisions.
9. Praise all successes.
10. Be genuinely concerned about the aspirations of the learner.

Identify training needs

Assess the skills and abilities of the learner against the requirements of the job

---

↓

Design, develop or plan the learning opportunity

- Identify the opportunities available to provide learning experiences for the learner
- Identify the most appropriate learning opportunity for the learner, taking into account the learner's preferred learning style

---

↓

Provide the learning opportunity

- Prepare the learner, brief them on what they will be expected to do
- Provide advice and support for the learner
- Encourage and praise the learner

↓

Evaluate the learning experience

- Was the learning activity successful?
- What has been learned?
- Are further opportunities required?

Figure 7.1 The coaching process

Demonstrations

Often a coach will be required to show the learner 'how to' perform a particular task. A good demonstration will not only clearly illustrate the particular skill, but will also outline the situations in which it should be used and the rationale for performing the skill in that particular way. It should highlight to the learner the importance of each stage and the reason why the skill is performed in that particular way. The coach takes the learner through each step, repeating steps if required until the learner is confident to perform the activity.

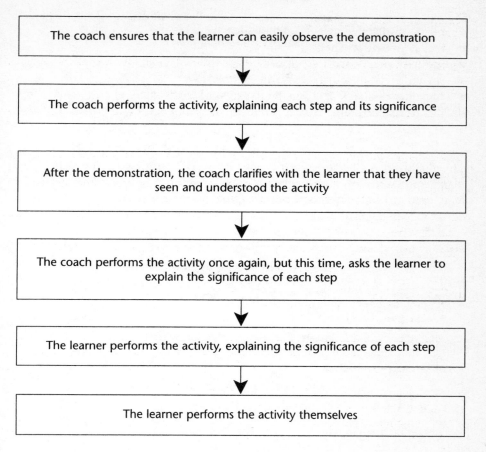

Figure 7.2 Coaching: a typical demonstration

Evaluation

The effect of any development activity is multiplied if the learner is aware of the process and its outcomes. Therefore, the evaluation of all development is crucial to coaching. Yet, evaluation should not be seen as something that is carried out at the end of the learning opportunity or activity, but something that should be structured into the way in which the development takes place.

In order to properly evaluate the learning outcomes of any learning opportunity both the learner and coach need to be clear from the outset what the learning needs or goals are, since the evaluation of the learning event is first and foremost an appraisal of the learning in relation to those learning goals. However, this should not be seen as the only outcome from the evaluation process. The evaluation process if it is conducted properly should also:

- refine and redefine the learner's learning needs
- motivate the learner
- identify new learning opportunities
- provide insights into working methods
- provide feedback on the effectiveness of work systems and procedures
- build a strong and trusting relationship between the coach and the learner.

The evaluation of the learning activity must begin with revisiting the learning goals which the activity was designed to meet. If those goals were the achievement of the occupational standards then a full evaluation could be an assessment against those standards.

Often the activity will be one of a series scheduled to develop competence and assessing the learner against the occupational standards may not be appropriate until after the series has been completed. However, an initial evaluation and its resultant feedback should be provided to the learner as soon after the activity as is practicable.

Table 7.2 Evaluation checklist

Evaluation checklist	Yes	No	Comments
What does the learner feel she has learned through the activity?			
Was the learning activity appropriate for the learning goal?			
How well does the learner feel she did?			
What has been learned?			
Has the development need been met?			
Could the learning activity be improved for future trainees?			
Was the learner provided with appropriate support?			
What are the implications for training and development within the organization?			

Without a structured recording mechanism, the longer term value of the evaluation will be lost. This is one of the reasons why organizations provide a formal structure for planning, recording and evaluating development activities. Sometimes this will be integrated with the appraisal system and sometimes it is separate, but whatever the mechanism it will enable the coach to identify appropriate training and development opportunities, record the training and development activities undertaken by the learner, and evaluate the effectiveness of the activity in meeting the development needs.

8

A Flexible Approach to Learning

Summary

In this chapter you will learn:

- how learning can be focused on the learner
- how to develop and use personal development plans
- what is meant by flexible learning materials
- how to develop flexible learning materials
- how colleagues can assist learners to use such material.

LEARNER-CENTRED LEARNING

As mentioned earlier, the motivation to learn rests with the learner. The learning organization can encourage that learning process through the nature of the activities made available and the attitude of their manager, supervisor or mentor. When learning is perceived to be interesting, fun, relevant and personally meaningful, then the learner will be motivated so long as they have control and influence over the learning process.

The learning organization should encourage a flexible, learner-centred approach to the acquisition of skills and abilities. Central to this approach is the personal development plan, where *individual* development needs are identified and *individual* solutions are designed to meet those needs. This has a number of advantages:

- only the specific development needs of the individual will be addressed. Hence, the learner will not have to waste time and effort attending training courses covering a wide range of skills and abilities which they already possess
- the developmental activity can be (at least partly) determined by the learner
- the timing of the developmental activity can be determined by the learner
- the evaluation criteria can also be determined by the learner.

This will ensure that the learner will view the activity as relevant, meaningful and under their control, thus encouraging committed and motivated learners. The only limit to the nature of the learning experience is the imagination of the learner (and possibly the resources available). The learner simply needs to show how the experience or activity will contribute towards the development of the particular skill or ability identified.

PERSONAL DEVELOPMENT PLANS (PDPS)

A PDP may be integrated into the organization's appraisal system or even form part of an NVQ assessment system but either way, it should form part of the planning process for learners' development. The PDP is a way of documenting the training and development objectives set by each learner and a way of monitoring progress towards meeting those objectives. It will provide the key mechanism to assist learners to keep up the momentum towards their development goals.

Although the format of a PDP may differ from one organization to another, it should include:

- the agreed training or development needs
- the performance goals of the learner
- the training and development methods to be employed
- the time-scale
- the evaluation or success criteria.

The PDP is where the learner has a chance to plan their learning. *They* determine where they feel that improvements can be made. *They* plan how those skills and abilities can be developed, and *they* monitor their progress. The PDP can focus the feedback from appraisals, assessments, or unsuccessful projects towards a positive outcome.

Although the goals laid out in the PDP are those of a particular learner, the input of their manager, supervisor or mentor will be crucial in focusing and guiding their priorities and options. The manager may be responsible for recommending and resourcing development activities. Acting as a coach, the manager may be the individual best placed to turn the plan into real learning opportunities. Either way, their input will be critical.

What should be in a PDP?

The first and crucial stage of any PDP is the assessment of skills and competence and the identification of the development needs. This may have been already identified through other mechanisms such as NVQ assessments, or performance appraisals. It could come from the learners themselves who feel that they are not competent in a particular area or they wish to develop particular skills and abilities so that they would be better placed for promotion or other changes in job roles and responsibilities.

A plan should motivate and encourage the learner as well as structure their development. In this sense it should be inspirational as well as aspirational, it should clearly link the needs of the learner on a personal and organizational level with their personal life goals. In this way the development can be seen to be relevant.

FLEXIBLE MATERIALS

A flexible approach to training and development activities would seem to necessitate a number of options for the learner. Although the coach can provide much needed one-to-one training and development as well as opportunities for experiential learning, this may not address the preferred learning style of all learners. The use of flexible training or learning materials may meet the needs of many learners. Indeed it is likely that learners will wish to take advantage of a number of different learning opportunities of which flexible learning materials are just one.

Open learning

Open and distance learning materials and programmes form a large part of learning provision in today's world and are widely and successfully used. Indeed, for many common skills and activities, open learning materials will be easily available and may provide a cost effective way of meeting particular development needs. However, the abundance of open learning materials means that there can be a great variation in the quality of the material. All open learning materials have one thing in common, they are designed to be used by people who have little or no access to a teacher or tutor. Hence, the materials are designed to provide all the assistance necessary to achieve the course objectives. Since there is no tutor available to explain, motivate, guide and appraise the learner, the materials themselves have to carry out these functions. Open and distance learning programmes are designed as an alternative to other forms of learning, but they are often most usefully used when combined and integrated with other methods.

Traditionally, open learning has been developed for academic qualifications and the vast majority of open learning programmes are designed to impart the knowledge required to achieve a particular academic qualification. It is only relatively recently that significant work has been done on competence-based or work-place-based open learning programmes.

The learning space

A learner's personal development is not generated from reading learning materials, and it does not come from the performance of the particular skill or ability, *it comes from the space in between*. It is important that the learner discovers each step in the learning process for themselves, that they unearth their own questions and find out their own answers on the way.

Good quality learning materials will empower the learner to establish for themselves the questions to be asked, the information that needs to be gathered and the answers that are appropriate. Good quality learning materials will show how aspects of skills and abilities can be practised in a safe environment. These activities would then grow in complexity as the materials moved the learner towards performing the skill or ability in a real situation or environment. Such materials are designed as a catalyst to the learning process rather than an instruction manual.

Flexible learning materials in the work-place

When learning materials are used to develop competence in a particular activity as opposed to simply imparting knowledge, they should function in a slightly different way from the more instruction-based, open learning materials. It is important that they make maximum use of the fact that the learner is in the work-place. This can be done only if the materials treat the work-place as a resource available to the learner.

Flexible learning designed to develop competence should:

- raise issues and questions which the learner can discuss and resolve through interaction with their colleagues
- encourage the learner to apply the ideas presented in the materials to their own work-place
- provide opportunities to undertake activities which will benefit the organization and the learner
- provide opportunities to produce evidence of competence (especially if the materials are to help the learner gain an NVQ or SVQ).

In common with other open learning materials, they should also:

- *Be structured to allow learners to access them at different points*. Some learners will wish to start at page one and work through the material in a linear fashion. Others may wish to go straight to the areas which interest them most. Others may wish to look at only the practical exercises. The materials should recognize the different ways they are likely to be accessed and provide clear signposting for the learner.

- *Contain lots of varied activities, clearly relevant to the learner's needs.* Variety in the materials will keep them fresh and exciting for the learner. If they are clearly relevant, the learner will be encouraged to know that they are learning and developing themselves.
- *Be visually stimulating and accessible.* If the materials look exciting it will encourage the learner to read on.
- *Address the candidate directly.* This will make the learner feel they are actively involved with the materials and not simply an observer.
- *Clearly and logically sequenced.* All learning materials need to be sequenced but this will be partly determined by the structure. There should be some variety in the sequencing of individual learning objectives within the materials. There should be a progression from simple ideas to complex ideas, from the known to unknown, and from the concrete to abstract. There may be other logical sequencing of learning points which may adhere to a causal, or a chronological sequence.

(If the materials were designed to develop competence to occupational standards it would also be worthwhile to show where activities may produce evidence of competence.)

Flexible learning materials should not aim to provide a comprehensive resource for the learner, but a stimulating and thought-provoking guide through all the main issues and controversies, not providing answers but directing questions.

As mentioned earlier, the materials are best used in conjunction with other learning or development activities. They work especially well as a guide for coaches or mentors, where the materials can be systematically worked through with the learner. In this way the materials can help structure the learning activities and provide a sequence for learning activities, with the coach or mentor used by the learner acting:

- as a sounding board where ideas and concepts are discussed
- as a supervisor to ensure that the activities are performed correctly
- as a coach to demonstrate competent performance.

LEARNING PROJECTS

A learning project is a way of systematically organizing 'informal, incidental, and formal learning activities conducted by a group of employees, around a central work related problem' (Poell *et al.*, 1997). Through working as a group to solve work related problems as part of a learning project, there are two main outcomes, improved competence and improved working methods. It is easy to see how learning projects are closely aligned to the principles of quality circles described in Chapter 6, and mirror them in many ways. Yet it would be wrong to assume that they are the same.

The learning project is set up specifically as a learning activity. The participants are actively involved in assisting each other to learn. They are aware of the learning process and may be involved to some degree with the experimentation and evaluation of learning and working methods but they are involved in the activity in order to improve their skills and abilities. The fact that the project involves solving a real work problem is only important in that it provides the mechanism to generate the learning.

Poell *et al.* (1997) identify four main characteristics of learning projects.

1. Learning together, where people learn from each other's experience and differing perspectives.
2. Conscious learning, where people are involved in the project with the sole intention of it providing a learning experience for them.
3. Multifaceted learning, where the project may include experimentation, training courses, research, and even involving external expertise.
4. Linking learning to work improvement, where the development of the new skills will enable the project participants to solve a particular problem *and* equip them to solve similar problems in the future.

Initiating learning projects

The learning project could be identified in a number of ways:

- through quality circles where a solution is identified but the skills to implement the solution do not exist within the organization
- a new method of working has been pioneered in another organization to considerable success, your organization wishes to implement this new method but there are no appropriately skilled personnel in the organization
- the organization is to engage in a new function and there are no appropriately skilled personnel in the organization
- a development need has been identified for a particular individual during the appraisal process and this activity has been identified by the employee as their preferred method of learning.

After agreeing the project and convening the group (all volunteers) the group should be left to determine how the project should be constructed, and how the problem will be solved. The group should be allocated reasonable resources to complete the project and provided with training and development expertise as required.

Learning projects can become a vital component of a healthy learning organization, they provide the clearest link between the organizational improvement through quality initiatives and organizational improvement through employee development.

9

THE LEARNING RESOURCE CENTRE

Summary

In this chapter you will learn about:

- how to set up a resource centre in an organization
- how to manage such a centre
- how to provide support for users of the centre.

A learning organization supports and encourages the individual development of staff. One of the key ways in which this can be put into action is through providing a sanctuary, away from the office or factory floor, where learning and development can take place. This learning resource centre should provide everything the staff would need to study and learn.

A learning resource centre can provide a focus for all training and development activity, helping to foster a learning culture. Although you may have a pre-conceived idea of what constitutes a learning resource centre, it is important to remember that the size, scope and make-up of a centre will differ depending upon the nature of the organization.

A learning resource centre will do more than simply provide a venue and resources for the development of individuals: it can also become a learning resource for the organization. It can contribute to an organizational memory. Individual learning experiences can be recorded and used as a resource for employees in the future, where learners will be able to learn from other people's mistakes rather than re-living the mistakes of the past.

MANAGEMENT OF THE LEARNING RESOURCE CENTRE

The key to the success of any learning resource centre is not the resources, materials and equipment supplied but the accessibility of the centre alongside the attitude of the employees to their personal development.

To maximize the usefulness of the resource centre it should be open, outside the organization's normal working hours, and during all breaks in the working day as a minimum. It should be sited so as to encourage access, possibly near to other staff facilities, and ideally not next to the managing director's office.

All learning resource centres will need to provide support in the use of the materials and equipment although the exact methods for doing this may differ between organizations. However, before many learners can master the intricacies of PCs, CD ROMs and the like, they will need support in study skills, so it is vital that the staff of the study centre are proactive. They should take time to understand and evaluate the needs of users and where appropriate offer advice and support to assist in the development of skills such as reading, taking notes, writing and the interpretation of statistics. The centre should have resources on hand to assist the learner with these skills but ideally the centre should provide access to personal tuition.

DESIGNING A LEARNING RESOURCE CENTRE

In planning a learning resource centre, the organization should examine the following:

- Demand: identify the different groups of learners that are likely to want to use the facility and why they would use it.
- Services: identify the types and nature of the services the centre will offer?
- Stake-holders: identify the requirements of the organization; what does the organization require of the centre.
- Performance or success standards: what will be used to measure the success or otherwise of the centre?
- Marketing: how will the centre attract users? How will they promote the benefits of the centre?
- Evaluation: how will the centre evaluate its services and the delivery of those services?
- Resources: identify the resources that will be available for the development of the centre.

The first step is to look at what is available locally at further and higher education institutions. Most of these institutions have resource centres and if there is a college nearby, it may make sense to come to an agreement with them to allow your staff to use their facilities. This would provide access to professional centre staff and expertise and could prove to be far more cost-effective than setting up an in-house centre. The logistics involved in using a college may prove to be a problem for many but should be examined. If you decide that an in-house centre is your preferred route you can still seek the advice of the staff of your local college resource centre who should be able to steer you away from any obvious pitfalls.

The learning resource centre, sited in an accessible position within the organization, should be well lit (preferably with at least some natural lighting) and ventilated. The make-up of every centre will differ to match the needs of the organization and the resources allocated to it. In determining the size of the centre, as a rule of thumb Julie Dorrell (1993) suggests accommodation for 25 per cent of staff that are within half an hour journey time of the centre. More equipment can be added later but extra space may not be as easy to add.

The main components of a LRC are as follows:

Workstations and furniture

- Desks and chairs where the desks are to hold computers as a workstation, the desks and chairs (typist's chairs) should be height adjustable wherever possible.
- Easy chairs and coffee tables should be used to mark off an area for browsing and taking a break.
- Screens should be used to separate some work-stations, especially where equipment is being used. This will help to minimize distractions and noise produced by the use of equipment.
- Table lamps should be available to provide some directed lighting.
- Notice board(s) should be used to pass on information to users of the centre.
- Shelving, cupboards and racks are essential for storing the different learning resources.

Equipment

- Multimedia personal computers (PCs) are essential and should be upgradeable and of the highest specification practicable. They should all include CD ROM drives and modems. It may prove useful to have a few portable laptop computers to loan staff members who need to do work at home. Before purchasing any PCs make sure that you have seen all the software which is to be used, working on that PC.
- Printer(s) are essential for all PC users. It may be worthwhile to let a number of the PCs share a printer or printers over a small network.
- Televisions and video cassette recorders for use mainly with training videos. However, more and more training and development is being made available through terrestrial (including digital), cable and satellite channels.
- CD and audio tape players.
- Headphones, these should be available for use with all relevant equipment, PCs, TVs and cassette recorders, etc.
- Photocopier.

Resources

- Books, periodicals and newsletters, relatively cheap, easy to store and can last.
- Videos, can be quite expensive, but can be used at home by most people. However, remember that they will degenerate over time.
- Audio cassettes, relatively cheap, small and very portable, most people have facilities to play them at home or in the car. Again, these tapes will degenerate over time.
- Compact disks and CD ROMs. CDs are widely used and most people will have facilities for playing them at home. Although CD ROMs that require a PC are not as widely used, if current projections are accurate, most homes will have a PC in the near future.
- Open/flexible learning materials, often a little expensive but extremely useful. Often incorporating other media such as videos, audio tapes and CDs, the materials are designed as a specific learning programme. Often, where specific learning materials or packs are being used, they have workbooks which are filled in by the user. If this is the case, numerous copies will need to be kept in stock or materials which include a photocopying agreement should be sought.
- Organizational information, such as reports, policies, procedures and publications.
- Computer software. More and more software is being developed to provide an interactive learning experience via the PC. Often this is in the form of a CD ROM but other technologies are and no doubt will continue to be used, especially via the Internet.
- Internet connection.
- Access to relevant cable, satellite and digital TV services.
- Training materials for the development of study skills.
- Expertise in using the resources.

These are the main items of furniture, equipment and resources that should be examined in relation to the needs of your learners. It is important to remember that as with all other work-stations, the facilities provided must conform to all relevant legislation, notably the Health and Safety at Work Act and Health and Safety (Display Screen Equipment) Regulations 1992.

It is important to recognize that there are health problems associated with computer work, especially where there is prolonged usage. The main problems are (a) fatigue and stress, (b) *temporary* eyestrain and headaches, and (c) upper limb disorders (pains in the neck, arms, elbows, wrists, hands, fingers). Reflections and glare on the screen should be avoided and work-stations should be assessed for risk. Users need to be trained in: how to adjust furniture to help avoid risks, how to organize the work-place to avoid repeated stretching movements, and the importance of good posture.

INDUCTION OF LEARNER TO THE RESOURCE CENTRE

The atmosphere and environment of the learning resource centre is crucial to its success. This is probably more so in a work-place, than it is in a place such as a public library. If we are to encourage potentially hesitant learners to take advantage of the services of the centre, we must not allow them any opportunity to walk away. The main instrument we have to foster an open and welcoming atmosphere is the staff of the resource centre.

Most public gyms will not allow people to enter for the first time without being shown around all the equipment first, many even require a rigorous assessment of their health and fitness prior to being allowed access to the gym. In many ways the learning resource is similar. When learners make use of the resource centre for the first time, the staff should evaluate the needs of the learner in terms of study support and also provide an induction for the learner. Some learners will be very sophisticated learners, others may have hardly ever been inside a library or learning resource centre and could require advice on:

- how they can determine their own information needs
- where different types of information are kept
- how to use catalogues and bibliographies
- copyright and photocopying
- where to go when the resource centre doesn't have what is required.

No matter how sophisticated a learner may be, if it is their first time in the resource centre, they will need advice on:

- the organization of the materials, the location of books, journals, magazines, audio cassettes, video cassettes, computer software
- the location of catalogues
- availability of material for lending
- where to get advice from subject specialists
- the use of any computerized information retrieval system
- opening times
- facilities and services for learners with special or particular needs
- what can and cannot be taken into and out of the centre
- how to use any installed equipment.

The most important message that must be communicated during this induction is a simple one. The learning resource staff have a primary role to help learners to obtain and gain the maximum use of the centres resources.

Linking learning to jobs

The learning organization should consider setting up a learning file for each employee or user of the centre, and a file for each job. The employee's learning file would include all the customary information relating to the learner (eg name, address, current job), as well as identified development needs. The file should also outline the different learning materials and strategies being employed to meet the development need.

Remember

A 'learning file' would provide ideal evidence for IiP indicator 3.6 (Chapter 10).

The job learning file should include an appraisal of all the beneficial learning experiences engaged in by the job incumbent and importantly, an assessment by the learner of the effectiveness of the materials. The evaluation of the materials should also be used by the staff of the resource centre to plan the acquisition of materials and the promotion of different learning strategies. The job learning file would stay with the job helping new incumbents to plan learning activities and helping to develop an organizational memory.

Remember

A 'job learning file' would provide ideal evidence for IiP indicator 4.2 (Chapter 10).

PART 3: GAINING RECOGNITION

The following chapters will show how as a learning organization, the organization is operating in a manner that will make it relatively easy to gain recognition for itself and the learners within it. The achievement of these particular standards, not only provides national recognition, but more importantly enables the organization to judge its own progress against those of its competitors. Moreover, some standards such as Investors in People actually help to structure the development of learners within organizations and as such, they help to structure the operations of a modern learning organization.

10

INVESTORS IN PEOPLE

Summary

In this chapter you will learn about:

- the IiP standard
- how a learning organization can achieve the standard.

THE INVESTORS IN PEOPLE STANDARD

The Investors in People (IiP) standard is awarded to organizations who can demonstrate that they can:

- set goals and objectives for the organization
- communicate those goals throughout the organization
- develop employees to meet the challenges of those goals

Any organization striving to become a learning organization should be well on the way to meeting this particular standard. Taking the three aspects of IiP as described above, it is easy to see how a learning organization should be able to demonstrate that it has achieved the standard. Moreover, the IiP standard provides the final link in the chain for the learning organization. It provides a validated structure for the management, review and evaluation of the mechanisms which ensure the development of the organization's people. (The indicators (numbers in square brackets) identified in this chapter have been simplified. For a full description of all the indicators please see Appendix B.)

The system for investors is analogous to the other standards based systems such as the NVQ system. Just as with the NVQ system, the onus is on the organization to provide the evidence to an assessor that the standard has been met.

Figure 10.1 illustrates where evidence towards IiP criteria may be found within the development process.

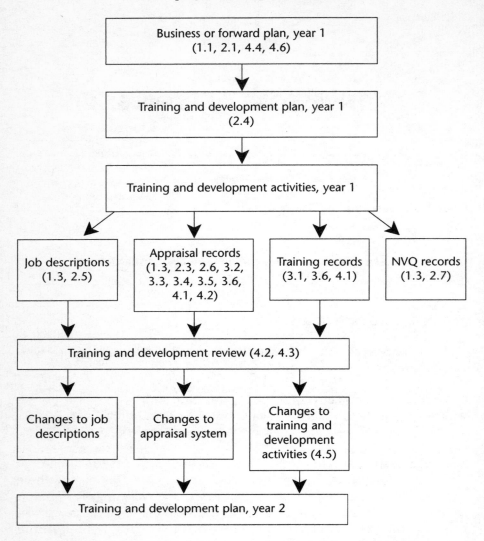

Figure 10.1 Where evidence towards IiP criteria may be found within the development process

THE FOUR PRINCIPLES

The IiP standard is in four sections:

- commitment
- planning
- action
- evaluation

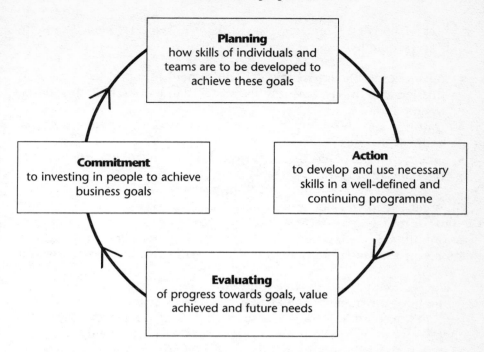

Figure 10.2 The four principles (© Investors in People UK 1998)

Commitment

An IiP organization must demonstrate a top-down commitment to develop all employees in order to achieve the organization's business objectives. To demonstrate this commitment an employer needs to show that:

[1.1] this commitment is communicated throughout the organization
[1.2] employees are aware of the broad aims or vision of the organization
[1.3] they have considered what the contribution is of all employees to the success of the organization, and those employees understand what is expected of them (see Chapter 2)
[1.4] where representative structures exist, these are used to communicate the vision and the contribution of employees.

A learning organization that has respect for the dignity of its employees should be able to effectively communicate its commitment as a learning organization to its employees. The assessor will look to see that the commitment is from the top and in action and deeds, not simply in writing. As mentioned previously, a learning organization is one where the whole culture and ethos of the organization revolves around the respect for, and development of, the work-force. Typical evidence for these indicators include:

- references to the organization's commitment to staff development in mission statements, business plans, staff handbooks, bulletins, newsletters [1.1]
- training and development plans, NVQ records, job descriptions, appraisal records [1.3]
- letters, minutes of meetings, agreements between employee representatives and the organization [1.4].

However, the main evidence of an organization's commitment will come from the staff. Employees at all levels need to believe that the organization is committed to their development. They need to be aware of the organization's mission and understand their contribution towards achieving that mission.

This will require an effective communication structure which operates throughout the organization at all levels. The assessor will be looking to see that the communication structure is not simply in place but that it is effective, or in other words the appropriate messages are being conveyed to staff at all levels and those staff are clear about what the organization expects of them.

This could lead to a few searching questions:

- How are the goals of the organization communicated?
- Is that communication effective, does it reach everyone with a consistent message?
- How are the concerns of employees communicated to management?
- Is that communication channel effective and are people encouraged to make use of it?

Answering these questions may identify areas where the organization needs to strengthen in order to achieve IiP status. As mentioned previously, a clear and effective communication system is crucial to any learning organization. The criterion that is used to evaluate if employees are aware of the broad aims or vision of the organization [1.2] is not assessing the employees *per se*, it is assessing the effectiveness of the communication system. However, it would be unusual if the assessor did not ask employees what they think the organization is trying to achieve and how the organization helps them to play their part in achieving the organization's mission. It is also not unheard of for the assessor to ask employees what they understand by the term 'investor in people'.

Planning

An IiP organization must demonstrate that they regularly review the development needs of employees and plan their training and development. To demonstrate a structured and planned response to the identification of training needs the employer needs to show that:

[2.1] they have a written plan setting out the organization's goals
[2.2] they have a written plan identifying training and development needs
[2.3] training and development needs are regularly reviewed at all levels
[2.4] they have a written plan identifying the resources for training
[2.5] the responsibility for training and development is clearly identified and understood
[2.6] objectives are set for training and development actions, at all levels
[2.7] if possible, training and development objectives are linked to external standards, such as NVQ or SVQs and occupational standards.

The majority of the evidence for these particular indicators can be wrapped up in two key documents, a business or forward plan which outlines the goals and targets of the organization and a training and development plan which will outline how training and development will help to achieve the business or forward plan. These plans need to be the product of a regular (usually annual) review process, where the plans are updated in line with what has been *learnt* during the previous year. (The training and development plan could form a part of the business or forward plan as a separate section and therefore one written plan could cover this section.)

The business plan should set out clearly the aims and objectives of the organization and outline the strategy that will be engaged to meet the goals and targets identified. It should also include a reference to training and development of staff and the resourcing of staff development activities, with all the appropriate budget information [indicators 2.1 and 2.4]. The training and development plan should demonstrate how the development of the human resources will contribute to the goals set out in the business plan.

These should:

- identify and review the training and development needs at the organization, and team level
- outline what actions are to be taken to meet those needs
- identify where the responsibility lies for training and development
- set objectives for the training and development actions at the organization and team level [indicators, 2.2, 2.5, 2.6].

If job descriptions of individuals who have a responsibility for developing employees accurately describe their job role, this will also provide good evidence towards indicator 2.5.

Alongside these pieces of evidence, there has to be some system of employee appraisal. This appraisal system should ensure that it follows on from and contributes to, the training and development plan. It should review the training and development needs of employees, and sets objectives for training and development goals for the individual [indicators 2.3, 2.6].

The assessor will be looking to see that these plans are implemented. If the plan refers to a budget for training and development they may look to see evidence of how it was spent. They may wish to trace this expenditure through the appraisal system to the learner's personal development plan.

Action

The IiP organization must demonstrate that it takes action to train and develop individuals within the organization. For a learning organisation, it should again be relatively easy to provide evidence that they can meet the following criteria:

[3.1] all new employees are effectively inducted to the organisation and the job
[3.2] managers are effective in training and developing employees
[3.3] managers support employees to meet their training and development needs
[3.4] all employees are made aware of the training and development opportunities open to them
[3.5] all employees are encouraged to help identify and meet their job-related development needs
[3.6] action takes place to meet all training and development needs.

If managers are responsible for assessing or coaching their staff, they will produce evidence of being involved and effective in the candidate's training and development [indicators 3.2 and 3.3]. Any appraisal system should provide ample evidence that employees are helped to identify their job-related training and development needs and are made aware of the development opportunities open to them [indicators 3.4 and 3.5]. If there is an effective induction programme *and* development activity is generated to meet the needs identified by the learner, and if this is in line with the requirements of the organizational plans, ample evidence should be available for the remaining indicators in this area [indicators 3.1 and 3.6].

Evaluation

Learning cannot happen without evaluation, hence it is no surprise that evaluation is central to the operation of all learning organizations. An IiP organization must evaluate the effectiveness of the training and development activities undertaken. It must assess how far the training and development activities have contributed to individuals' learning and implement improvements identified through the evaluation. An IiP organization must demonstrate that:

[4.1]   it evaluates the impact of training and development on knowledge, skills and attitude
[4.2]   it evaluates the impact of training and development on job performance
[4.3]   it evaluates the contribution of training and development to the achievement of its goals
[4.4]   top management understands the broad cost and benefits of training and developing employees
[4.5]   action takes place to implement improvements to training and development as a result of evaluation
[4.6]   top management's continuing commitment to training and developing employees is demonstrated to all employees.

The evaluation of training and development activities is carried out by many people at all levels of the organization – the coach or trainer, the learner, the organization as a whole. The IiP organization needs to demonstrate that training and development activities are evaluated for their effectiveness in meeting the identified need. One way would be to reassess the learner against the occupational standard, this could be as part of the appraisal system or as part of an NVQ assessment. This should provide a good evaluation of skills, knowledge and performance [indicators 4.1 and 4.2]. However, in terms of evidence, it should be remembered that without recording the evaluation it will be of limited worth. The results of the evaluation needs to be recorded in the learner's personal development plan.

11

NVQ/SVQ Assessment Centre Status

Summary

This chapter you will learn about:

- NVQs and SVQs

- identify the quality assurance systems and assessment criteria which are linked to achieving them

- how organizations can become approved assessment centres

- assessor training, centre management and internal verification.

National and Scottish Vocational Qualifications

National Vocational Qualifications (NVQs) and Scottish Vocational Qualifications (SVQs) are qualifications composed entirely of standards of occupational competence. Scottish Vocational Qualifications (SVQs) are to all intents and purposes identical to their NVQ equivalent. The only real difference is that SVQs may reflect slight differences in terms of legal requirements and procedures within Scotland. SVQs are mainly available in Scotland, and NVQs mainly available in the rest of the UK. For this reason I will refer only to NVQs, but all references to NVQs can be read as for SVQs.

The qualifications are constructed so as to appeal to particular occupational groups. Consequently, if you have identified a number of occupational standards for the training and development of certain individuals in your organization, there could quite possibly be an NVQ which will cover their job role. However, it is only fair to add the warning that there is not likely to be an exact match between job-roles and NVQs. This is of course not surprising if we look at the scope and remit of qualifications.

NVQs are designed to appeal to all the employees who are performing the same job role in different organizations throughout the land. That means that the qualification is looking to be equally as valid to large private sector organizations as it is to small public sector ones and, as if this isn't enough, it needs to be valid to post-holders who operate with very different job descriptions, levels of responsibility and autonomy. As a result, many NVQs will ask more of employees than is strictly required by their organization. This could be viewed in a number of ways. It could be that the organization accepts that the acquisition of NVQs would make the employees more skilled and possibly anticipate a development of their job role. It could be seen by the organization that the achievement of NVQs will demonstrate to the outside world that the organization not only operates to the national standards but also that they meet the rigorous quality standards set by the awarding body and ultimately the Qualification and Curriculum Authority (QCA) (in Scotland, the Scottish Qualifications Authority (SQA)). It may be seen by the organization that the provision of NVQs to their staff represents a reward to the staff for all their hard work in developing themselves. However, it should be recognized that it may not be of immediate benefit to the organization, indeed, it may make the employee more employable to a future employer.

In order for an individual to achieve one of these qualifications they must demonstrate to an approved assessor that they have met all the standards that constitute the qualification in question. The quality of the assessment process is assured by having all assessors operate within approved centres. These centres are in turn monitored by awarding bodies, who are themselves monitored and approved by the accrediting bodies (QCA for NVQs and SQA for SVQs). In this system, the awarding bodies stipulate a set of criteria that all potential assessment centres must meet before they can be approved. Once approved, the awarding body will monitor the assessment process, the quality of the assessments and the management of the centre, usually through regular visits by awarding body representatives. The accrediting bodies in turn approve and monitor awarding bodies to guarantee that they are ensuring the quality of the qualifications through effective implementation of centre approval and verification regimes. The last few years have seen a move by the accrediting bodies to standardize the delivery system by agreeing with awarding bodies a set of guiding principles, or a model of good practice called The Common Accord.

QUALITY ASSURANCE SYSTEMS

Organizations that wish to be approved to offer NVQs must demonstrate to the awarding body that they have systems in place to deliver consistent NVQ assessments. The awarding body will be looking for evidence that the organization has:

- adequate management systems
- adequate resources
- support for candidates
- effective assessment and verification systems
- adequate documentation systems
- effective review procedures.

Although each awarding body may still have slightly different criteria, they will shortly be required to use the criteria determined by The National Council for Vocational Qualifications. NCVQ was the organization responsible for NVQs prior to its merger with the School Curriculum and Assessment Authority (SCAA) to form QCA in 1997.) Accordingly, the advice contained within this chapter relates to these criteria which are reproduced in full as Appendix C. (The SQA will be issuing their own approved centre criteria for centres wishing to offer SVQs although the criteria may differ slightly in actual wording to those produced by NCVQ, the areas of approval will remain the same.)

The responsibility lies with the organization to demonstrate that they have all the systems, procedures, staff and commitment to make it happen. The nature of criterion based referencing systems means that it will allow a great deal of flexibility in how this evidence can be put together. Yet rarely do awarding bodies provide clear guidance on how most organizations would want to present that evidence. What follows is a step-by-step example of how an assessment centre can be structured, *it is not the only way*.

How organizations can become approved assessment centres

First, whatever the nature of the organization it is important to remember that the awarding body and the awarding body staff will only be interested in how your organization meets the approval criteria. Anything that is included in your application which does not directly demonstrate how the organization meets the approval criteria serves only to confuse and obscure the application.

Second, awarding bodies produce application forms for good reasons. Always fill in the application in full if you have been supplied with one. The completed application form will serve as a narrative on which to hang the actual evidence. Simply referencing evidence to sections of the application form will not be sufficient as it will not assist in arriving at a common understanding of the adequacy of the evidence you are presenting.

Your responsibility is not just to supply the evidence, but to supply it in such a manner as to make it comprehensible to awarding body representatives. A badly constructed application containing large amounts of irrelevant information is likely to raise questions with the awarding body about the organization's ability to assess evidence presented by candidates.

What follows is a step-by-step guide to becoming an assessment centre for one organization with a number of sites. When designing and planning an NVQ centre refer to the *approved centre criteria* (see Appendix C) to ensure that all the criteria are being met. Although these steps are in a logical sequence there is nothing to stop some of the steps being performed concurrently.

Step 1
Write a forward plan which clearly describes:

- the NVQ centre, the lines of communication and authority [1.1.3]
- the make-up and frequency of the NVQ centre management group
- the centre's aims and objectives and a development timetable [1.1.1]
- the level of resources allocated for the centre [1.2.1], [1.2.3], [1.2.5]
- the centre's policies (e.g. fair assessment, health and safety, staff development) [1.1.2], [1.2.2], [1.2.4]

Step 2
This plan should be approved by senior management and there should be documentation to that effect (eg Minutes of a board meeting). [1.1.1]

Step 3
The operation of the centre will be managed and reviewed by a centre management group which will meet at least annually. The management group will normally include all internal verifiers, at least one assessor, and the centre contact. The centre management group will have the authority to change or amend the centre plan. [3.2.4], [3.2.3], [3.2.2]

Step 4
Document the internal verification procedure for the centre. This could form part of the forward plan possibly as an annex. [1.1.4]

What follows is an outline of procedures which should meet the assessment and internal verification requirement of the approval criteria. Of course the real task is to operate consistently to this level of quality.

The internal verifier will be an individual who has either achieved the qualification they are to verify or has other qualifications and/or experience which meet all the awarding bodies criteria for occupational competence. The internal verifier will either hold the units D32 and D33 or will have been on a recognized training course covering the assessor units D32 and D33. The internal verifier will hold the unit D34 or will have received training *and* be actively working towards achieving the unit D34 within 12 months of commencing internal verification duties. [2.2.5]

Verification in the context of NVQs and SVQs means the monitoring of assessment practice, confirming the assessment decisions, and ensuring assessments are in line with the national standards and those of the awarding body.

The internal verifier will:

- allocate candidates to assessors
- verify the work of all allocated assessors
- verify 100 per cent of assessments carried out by assessors who have not achieved D32 and D33
- verify a minimum of 15 per cent of assessments carried out by assessors who hold D32 and D33
- identify inconsistencies of assessment [2.2.4]
- provide constructive and supportive feedback to assessors to ensure consistency of assessment [2.2.4]
- act on the advice provided by the allocated external verifier [3.2.1]
- appropriately record all verification activity [3.1.2]
- ensure that they work to the standard of unit D34 [2.2.5]
- ensure that the centre's quality assurance program is implemented
- preside over appeals according to the centre's appeals procedure.

In addition to their internal verification work they will act as a formal adviser to candidates. The internal verifier will facilitate candidate forums where candidates will work cooperatively to develop skills and collect evidence. [2.1.1], [2.1.3]

The assessor will be an individual who has either achieved the qualification or has other qualifications and/or experience which meet all the awarding bodies' criteria for occupational competence. The assessor will either hold the units D32 and D33 or will have received training *and* be actively working towards achieving the units D32 and D33 within 12 months of commencing assessor duties. [2.2.3]

The assessor will:

- plan the development and assessment of candidates [2.1.2], [2.1.3]
- appropriately assess all allocated candidates [2.1.4], [2.2.1]
- judge evidence presented by candidates against the national standards
- determine when a candidate has achieved the qualification
- appropriately record all assessment and planning activities [2.1.2], [2.1.3], [3.1.1], [3.1.4]
- act on the advice provided by the internal verifier [2.2.4], [3.2.1]
- ensure that they work to the standard of D32 and D33 [2.2.1]

Internal verification meetings will take place every month on the third Wednesday of the month at 1.00pm. These meetings will be attended by the internal verifier, all assessors and if requested, the centre contact. The assessors will bring all evidence produced by their allocated candidates which has not been verified by the internal verifier. The internal verification meetings will be supplemented by the observation of assessors assessing candidates. The internal verification meetings will be the main opportunity for the execution of all verification activities.

This will be the formal forum for discussing the evidence presented by candidates with other assessors and the internal verifier. This forum is there to provide advice, guidance, support and verification for assessors. Each meeting will have a standard agenda to ensure that all critical areas are covered. Each meeting will be minuted, and minutes will be sent to all members within 14 days. [3.1.2]

The standard agenda will include the following headings:

- health and safety issues arising from assessment activities [1.2.2]
- access and fair assessment issues arising from assessment activities
- interpretation of standards [2.2.2]
- resource or equipment needs [1.2.1]
- and how they will be met
- candidate assessment needs [2.1.4]
- candidate training and development needs [2.1.2]
- verification of assessments [2.2.4]
- units verified and recommended for certification [2.2.7]
- changes to the assessment team [2.2.6]
- correspondence with awarding body [2.2.2], [2.2.6]
- the effectiveness of the internal verification meetings and suggestions for improvement.

The centre contact will liaise with the awarding body to ensure that the centre continues to meet the approval criteria. They will register all candidates with the awarding body and notify the awarding body of any certification required. They will also provide a secure and confidential recording system. [3.1.1]

This will store up to date:

- minutes of all internal verification meetings [3.1.2]
- correspondence with the awarding body [1.1.5], [3.1.3]
- registration and certification information [3.1.1], [3.1.3]
- candidate records, including portfolios/evidence that has been requested for external verification purposes [3.1.1]
- information relating to the access and fair assessment policy, including details of registration and certification rates in relation to factors such as ethnic origin, gender, disability, etc. [3.1.4]

Ratios of candidates to assessors will be of the order of 4:1, so that no assessor will have responsibility for more than four candidates at any one time. The ratio of assessors to internal verifiers will be 8:1, so that no internal verifiers will have responsibility for more than eight assessors at any one time. These ratios will be seen as the norm but will be subject to periodic review by the centre management group.

The candidate appeals procedure (see Figure 11.1), will be distributed to all candidates prior to them embarking upon the qualification. All candidates will be asked to read the procedure in the presence of the assessor and clarify with the assessor any areas which they do not understand. [2.1.5]

Step 5
Identify and recruit all centre staff. [1.2.3]

Step 6
Train all staff members to the relevant D units they are required to possess or be trained in and induct all staff in the procedures and systems for delivering assessment and verification. [1.2.4]

Step 7
Identify, recruit and induct candidates.

Step 8
Operate the centre according to the forward plan and the internal verification procedures.

Running an assessment centre

Verifying assessments

Verification of assessments falls into two parts: the examination of the (i) assessment process – the activities of the assessor and their planning, organization and feedback skills and (ii) assessment products – portfolios, evidence and the candidate.

When examining the assessment process, the internal verifier should ask a number of questions:

- Is the assessor providing an adequate level of support for the candidate?
- Is the assessor meeting the timetable agreed with the candidate?
- Is the assessor assessing candidates consistently?
- Is the assessor asking more of the candidate that what is required by the standards?
- Is the assessor recording assessments activities appropriately?

Candidate appeals procedure

---

1. Any candidate who feels that their NVQ or SVQ assessment has been unfairly assessed can appeal against the decision of an assessor. For an appeal to be eligible the candidate must:
   - explain to the assessor why they feel they have been unfairly assessed
   - provide the assessor with the evidence they have for arriving at that decision
   - raise the matter with the assessor within 14 days of the original decision.

   The assessor and candidate will arrive at a mutually agreed resolution to the appeal.
2. If the assessor and the candidate cannot arrive at a mutually agreed resolution, the assessor will notify (in writing) the internal verifier within seven days.
3. The internal verifier will investigate the appeal and arrive at a resolution acceptable to the candidate. If this is not possible, the internal verifier will notify the external verifier (in writing) within 14 days.
4. The external verifier at her next scheduled visit, will investigate the appeal and arrive at a resolution. The candidate is entitled to put their case to the external verifier face to face. The external verifier's decision is final.
5. Only if a candidate believes that *these procedures* are not being observed by the assessor can she contact the internal verifier directly. Likewise, only if a candidate believes that *these procedures* are not being observed by the internal verifier can she contact the internal verifier directly, and only if she believes that *these procedures* are not being observed by the internal verifier may she contact the awarding body directly. In every case the candidate must provide evidence of a breakdown in the procedure.

Figure 11.1 Example of appeals procedure

When examining the assessment products the verifier must ask the following questions:

- Is the most appropriate evidence being targeted?
- Is maximum use being made of evidence?
- Are assessor records, complete, accurate, brief and readable?
- Is the evidence, authentic, current, reliable and sufficient?
- Is the evidence valid, does it clearly show that the standard has been achieved?

NVQ/SVQ *assessment centre status*

Candidate		Evidence reference			
Assessor		Unit/elements reference			
Is the evidence ...				**Yes**	**No**
... authentic, is it obviously the product of the candidate?					
... the most appropriate for the candidate?					
... complete?					
... reliable?					
... sufficient to cover all the pcs?					
... current?					
Does the evidence ...					
... cover all range and knowledge statements?					
... meet the evidence requirements?					
Are all assessor records ...					
... full?					
... legible?					
Comments:					
Signed:			**Date:**		

Figure 11.2 Example of verification checklist

131

- Is the evidence easy to locate?
- Is there adequate performance *and* knowledge evidence?

Simple checklists such as Figure 11.2 are often used by verifiers as an *aide-mémoir* to ensure that they have covered all the ground. This will have a second and possibly more significant purpose of providing documentary evidence to any external verifier that this checking has been done.

Sampling

When sampling evidence, the verifier is taking a random sample of the available evidence from candidates. Yet by carefully structuring the sample, the verifier can provide data on the assessment decisions:

- by experienced/inexperienced assessors – for the same candidates; for the same units
- based on different methods of assessment for the same units
- recorded in different ways
- arrived at by differing amounts of evidence.

The data supplied by such sampling should lead to developing a guide to best practice which can assist assessors in how to conduct the most cost-effective and accurate assessment, thereby, ensuring that the organization learns from the activities of verification.

12

ISO 9000, BS5750 AND TOTAL QUALITY MANAGEMENT

Summary

In this chapter you will learn about:

- the benefits of quality standards
- Implementing ISO 9000 and BS5750
- total quality management.

Learning organizations are, by definition, on a constant drive to improve their effectiveness and hence improve the quality of their goods or services. Quality initiatives can provide a focus or channel for the efforts of the learning organization.

ISO 9000

ISO 9000 certification is rapidly becoming a key factor in creating a competitive edge. An increasing number of European companies have for some time required ISO certification of their suppliers. The desire to sell products in Europe has led to an expansion in its use across the USA and is now the international standard in every sense. Even NASA has adopted ISO 9000 as the basis for its quality system and the quality systems of its suppliers.

What is ISO 9000 and BS 5750?

ISO 9000 is a formal management system that has been designed to be adapted to an individual organization's needs. ISO 9000 is an internationally recognized standard but is also known as BS 5750 in the UK (and even EN 29000 in the EC). Quite simply, ISO 9000 requires an organization to:

- document its systems and procedures
- monitor those systems and procedures to encourage consistent compliance
- be audited by a certification body.

In other words, you say what you are going to do, you do it, then you prove that you have done it. Of course, just as with occupational standards, the organization could make use of the standard without being audited and therefore not receive a certificate. Yet most organizations want to have something to show for all their hard work and wish to demonstrate to others that they have met the ISO 9000 standard.

The standard is in two main parts. ISO 9001 (BS 5750 part 1) is for organizations whose customers expect them to design products or services specially for them. ISO 9002 (BS 5750 part 2) is for organizations who produce standard goods or services. The nature of the organization should determine which standard to use.

An organization that can achieve the ISO 9000 standard could:

- improve customer satisfaction, *leading to* better customer loyalty and reducing customer dissatisfaction
- reduce costs *because* less resources are spent on reworking, eliminating scrap and reducing customer support and service costs
- open up new markets *because* less resources are spent on reworking, eliminating scrap and reducing customeer support and service costs
- open up new markets *because* they become eligible as a supplier to organizations that require ISO 9000 compliance.

Although the standard was designed to meet the needs of manufacturers it is equally applicable to service organizations. The language of the standard does put off some organizations because it refers to products and not services, but for ISO 9000, service *is* a product.

For a learning organization that is consistently evaluating and making improvements to performance, the application of ISO 9000 can help to focus the efforts of the organization in assuring the quality of the organization, not simply in terms of its operation but also in terms of its implementation.

The concept

ISO 9000 is based upon a number of assumptions. It assumes that the quality of an organization's product (or service) can be influenced by:

- management
- policies and procedures
- design
- training
- customers
- technologies
- work practices
- work monitoring
- resources allocated
- job descriptions
- planning practices
- inspection and testing systems
- production processes
- appraisal relationships
- communication patterns
- transportation
- record keeping systems
- service delivery practices
- inventory control methods
- employee knowledge and skill.

ISO 9000 looks to control all these influences to ensure that the organization has control over the quality of its product or service. ISO 9000 looks at the qualities or *characteristics* of the organization that may influence product quality. The standard specifies the general qualities that your products or services should have. For instance, they should be properly designed, stored, delivered, installed and serviced. It leaves it up to the organization to determine the specific qualities.

Implementing the standard

It is essential that an implementation programme *management commitment*, this can be reinforced and encouraged by identifying the benefits. In order to identify the benefits the current situation needs to be accurately assessed. All the costs associated with poor quality should be identified as well as all the opportunities for the organization in terms of future customers and new markets. This should be balanced with costs involved in implementing a quality programme, the present state of the organization's documentation, how much external assistance will be needed and how much reorganization and staff development is likely to be needed.

Only after that stage has been completed can the implementation plan be prepared. Kit Sadgrove (1994) identifies the seven underlying principles of ISO 9000:

1. be organized (have an organization chart outlining roles and responsibilities)
2. work to written procedures
3. control key documents
4. keep records
5. carry out regular checks
6. identify faults and correct them
7. communicate well

This is what an organization has to do to achieve the standard. The way that the organization does these seven things is to a large extent up to them. ISO 9000 is only concerned with determining whether or not organization does what it says that it does. So in essence, ISO 9000 asks an organization to provide a description of what they do, and that description must address all the issues outlined in the full standard (for a full summary of the standard see Appendix D), the certification body will check to see that the organization's practices are consistent with the description.

Systems manuals

One of the main tasks for most organizations wishing to achieve ISO 9000 is the documenting of the organization's systems and procedures, usually involving the production of systems and procedures manuals. The objective of these manuals is to document all the systems and procedures that have a direct effect on quality.

The way that an organization develops these manuals and the number and scope of these manuals is left up to each organization to determine. What does need to be clear is the relationship of one manual to another and each manual's relationship to the quality policy of the organization.

As mentioned previously, a learning organization needs to be able to adapt its systems and procedures as required. This should be borne in mind when developing the manuals and this usually means that the manuals are produced in ring binders so that updating can be done easily. For an example of a specimen procedure see Figure 3.1.

Time spent developing the structure of the procedures, the manuals and the system for updating and changing different aspects is always time well spent. Many organizations develop their systems and procedures with modern word processing programmes. Most can automate and systematize a great deal of the production and amendment of procedures. Often (sometimes with the help of some very simple macros) they can:

- protect documents, only allowing certain personnel to make changes
- identify other related documents which may need to be amended as a result of the change
- provide a list of people who need to be informed of any changes
- identify the number and location of all manuals that need updating
- automatically number documents.

Manuals should be organized in a logical pattern, often with different sections relating to different departments, or job roles. Copies of all forms referred to in the manuals should be either available in the manual or form part of a forms and records manual.

There are many advantages of a documented quality management system, it enables the organization to:

- promote 'best practice'
- determine and put right the activities which lead to poor quality
- encourage consistency
- audit and monitor quality activities.

In a learning organization the manuals should be easily accessible and used regularly. They will form a crucial part in helping new staff to fully understand their job role, and form a resource for all staff who may not be clear about what they are expected to do.

Internal auditing

Internal auditing of the quality systems is the organization's main method of ensuring that the system works properly. It is the way in which problems can be identified and resolved and it is a way of assessing whether or not previous amendments actually work.

To perform an audit the organization needs to;

- *Determine who will act as the auditors*. For instance, the auditors should not be involved in the process they are auditing and the organization needs to determine how many auditors will be required.
- *Train the auditors*. Where auditors have not had experience or training in auditing, they will require training, such as that of the National Registration Scheme for Assessors of Quality Systems.
- *Produce an audit plan*. This will identify which departments are to be audited, the scope of the audit, the auditor and the planned date of the audit.

The skills of an auditor are similar to those of an assessor as discussed in Chapter 5. However, the application of those skills is different. Where an assessor is trying to determine whether the quality of performance has met the performance standards, the auditor is trying to determine if the documented procedures are being carried out and documented.

The auditor must ensure that every audit is documented, and a report is produced. Where problems are identified the auditor should determine the cause of the problem, produce a non-conformance report and agree corrective action. The reports should then be made available for the departments concerned. Once the organization is confident that its systems and procedures are effective, it is in a position to be registered. This is done by contracting with a certification body to assess your system, if the system passes then the organization receives an ISO 9000 certificate.

TOTAL QUALITY MANAGEMENT

Total quality management (TQM) is a term initially coined by the US Naval Air Systems Command to dèscribe its Japanese-style management approach to quality improvement. Since then, TQM has taken on many meanings, but basically, TQM is a management approach to long-term success through customer satisfaction. It is based on the participation of all members of an organization in improving processes, products, services, and the culture they work in.

Often seen as an alternative to ISO 9000, it is probably more accurate to see it as the next step up the quality ladder. Its aim is the same as ISO 9000, continual improvement through improved quality, however unlike ISO 9000 where the quality standard itself drives a compliance programme, with TQM it is customers that drive the quality improvement programme. Not just external customers, people who want to purchase goods and services from you but *internal customers* within organizations.

For TQM, the quality of a product or service is determined by customer expectations. The quality of a product is the customer's perception of the degree to which the product or service meets her expectations. The significance of using customers as a measure of the quality of the product is simple, the satisfaction of the customer has a direct relationship with the profitability of the organization, and hence the success of the organization.

TQM is not a standard like ISO 9000 or IiP, it is an approach to the way that organizational development and HRD can be focused to continually learn and improve through meeting and surpassing customer needs. It is easy to see how the approach of TQM is consistent with that of a learning organization.

TQM is not, however, simply a case of exhorting employees to identify and act on quality related issues. The organization has to develop mechanisms to enable the TQM process. It is about creating a quality culture building a *shared* vision of the organization's goals. Quality is a long-term goal, staff should be motivated and developed over a long period of time, continual training and development is crucial to support the quality culture. The main elements of the TQM culture are:

- commitment from management *and* employees
- customer involvement in all aspects of quality from design to after sales support
- products *designed* and *controlled* for quality
- processes *designed* and *controlled* for quality
- empowered employees
- partnerships with suppliers
- decisions based on evidence
- cooperative relationships

Much of the writing on TQM stresses many of the issues central to the concept of the learning organization with one main focus – the customer. In TQM, there is an important correlation between satisfying internal customers and meeting external customers needs. In other words if you do not treat your employees with respect and satisfy their needs, it is not surprising if they treat customers in the same way. Not surprisingly, the reverse is also true. The TQM organization in common with the learning organization should treat its employees in the same way that it would like its customers to be treated.

APPENDIX A: COMPANY APPRAISAL SYSTEM

Post: Junior Management Consultant   Date: [　　　　　　　　]

Appraisee: [　　　　　　　　　　　]

Appraiser: [　　　　　　　　　　　]

The appraisal will be based on performance against the standards and goals outlined below.

Competence standards for the post

1. Manage activities to meet customer requirements (MCI, unit A3)
2. Facilitate meetings (MCI, unit D2)
3. Provide information to support decision-making (MCI, unit D4)
4. Manage continuous quality improvement (MCI, unit F3)
5. Plan and prepare projects (MCI, unit G4)
6. Manage the running of projects (MCI, unit G6)
7. Complete projects (MCI, unit G6)
8. Manage the use of financial resources (MCI, unit B3)
9. Communicate with customers (CSLB)
10. Solve problems on behalf of customers (CSLB)

Goals agreed from previous action plan

Competence standards assessed this year	Competent
_____	Yes/No
_____	Yes/No
_____	Yes/No
_____	Yes/No

Which of the identified goals for this year do you believe that you achieved or exceeded?

Appraisee

Of the remaining goals, why were they not achieved satisfactorily?

Appraisee

Have there been any situations or incidents which have a bearing upon your performance during this year?

Appraisee

What lessons have been learned from this year? How can they be put into effect in the coming year to improve your performance?

Appraisee

How has training or development activity affected your performance?

Appraisee

What is your assessment of the appraisee's general performance for the previous year?

Appraiser

What specific areas of performance have not lived up to expectations?

Appraiser

Are there areas where you feel that you would benefit from specific training?

Appraiser

How could these areas be improved in the coming year?

Appraiser

What areas of the appraisee's performance exceeded your expectations?

Appraiser

How can these achievements be built on in the coming year?

Appraiser

What competence standards will be assessed during the next year?

Appraiser

What training and development is required?

Training and development	*Completed by*
Appraiser	

What are the *agreed goals* for the next year?

Appraiser

Appraisee:

Appraiser:

Date:

Appendix B:
The IIP Standard

The Investors in People Standard is protected by intellectual property rights under national and international law. The Standard may not be reproduced in whole or in part without prior written consent from Investors in People UK. Unauthorized copying is actionable under both civil and criminal legislation.

Commitment

An investor in people makes a commitment from the top to develop all employees to achieve its business objectives.

Indicators

1.1 The commitment from top management to train and develop employees is communicated effectively throughout the organization.
1.2 Employees at all levels are aware of the broad aims or vision of the organization.
1.3 The organization has considered what employers at all levels will contribute to the success of the organization, and has communicated this effectively to them.
1.4 Where representation structures exist, communication takes place between management and representatives on the vision of where the organization is going and the contribution employees and their representatives will make to its success.

Planning

An investor in people regularly reviews the needs and plans the training and development of all employees.

Indicators

2.1 A written but flexible plan sets out the organization's goals and targets.

2.2 A written plan identifies the organization's training and development needs, and specifies what actions will be taken to meet these needs.
2.3 Training and development needs are regularly reviewed against goals and targets at the organization, team and individual level.
2.4 A written plan identifies the resources that will be used to meet training and development needs.
2.5 Responsibility for training and developing employees is clearly identified and understood throughout the organization, starting at the top.
2.6 Objectives are set for training and development actions at the organization, team and individual level.
2.7 Where appropriate, training and development objectives are linked to external standards, such as National Vocational Qualifications (NVQs) and Scottish Vocational Qualifications (SVQs) and units.

ACTION

An investor in people takes action to train and develop individuals on recruitment and throughout their employment.

Indicators

3.1 All new employees are introduced effectively to the organization and all employees new to a job are given the training and development they need to do that job.
3.2 Managers are effective in carrying out their responsibilities for training and developing employees.
3.3 Managers are actively involved in supporting employees to meet their training and development needs.
3.4 All employees are made aware of the training and development opportunities open to them.
3.5 All employees are encouraged to help identify and meet their job-related training and development needs.
3.6 Action takes place to meet the training and development needs of individuals, teams and the organization.

EVALUATION

An investor in people evaluates the investment in training and development to assess achievement and improve future effectiveness.

Indicators

4.1 The organization evaluates the impact of training and development actions on knowledge, skills and attitude.
4.2 The organization evaluates the impact of training and development actions on performance.
4.3 The organization evaluates the contribution of training and development to the achievement of its goals and targets.
4.4 Top management understands the broad cost and benefits of training and developing employees.
4.5 Action takes place to implement improvements to training and development identified as a result of evaluation.
4.6 Top management's continuing commitment to training and developing employees is demonstrated to all employees.

Appendix C:
Approved Centre Criteria

1 Planning

Management systems

Criteria

1.1.1 The centre's aims and policies in relation to NVQs and plans for their achievement are supported by senior management and understood by the assessment team.
1.1.2 The centre's access and fair assessment policy and practice is understood and complied with by candidates and assessors.
1.1.3 The roles, responsibilities, authorities and accountabilities of the assessment and verification team across all assessment sites are clearly defined, allocated and understood.
1.1.4 Internal verification procedures and activities are clearly documented, consistent with national requirements and ensure the quality and consistency of assessment.
1.1.5 There is effective communication within the assessment team and the awarding body.

Resources

Criteria

1.2.1 Resource needs are correctly and accurately identified in relation to the specific award and resources are made available.
1.2.2 Equipment and accommodation used for the purposes of assessment comply with the requirements of relevant health and safety acts.
1.2.3 There are sufficient competent and qualified assessors and internal verifiers to meet the demand for assessment and verification activity.
1.2.4 A staff development programme is established for the assessment and verification team in line with identified needs.
1.2.5 Assessors and verifiers have sufficient time, resources and authority to perform their roles and responsibilities effectively.

2 DELIVERY

CANDIDATE SUPPORT

Criteria

2.1.1 Information, advice and guidance about the qualification procedures and practices are provided to candidates and potential candidates.
2.1.2 Candidates' development needs are matched against the requirements of the award and an agreed individual assessment plan is established.
2.1.3 Candidates have regular opportunities to review their progress and goals and to revise their assessment plan accordingly.
2.1.4 Particular assessment requirements of candidates are identified and met wherever possible.
2.1.5 There is an established appeals procedure which is documented and made available to all candidates.

ASSESSMENT AND INTERNAL VERIFICATION

Criteria

2.2.1 Access to assessment is encouraged through the use of a range of valid assessment methods.
2.2.2 Queries about the qualification specification, assessment guidance or related awarding body material are resolved and recorded.
2.2.3 Assessment is conducted by qualified and occupationally expert staff.
2.2.4 Assessment decisions and practices are regularly sampled and findings are acted upon to ensure consistency and fairness.
2.2.5 Internal verification is conducted by appropriately qualified and experienced staff.
2.2.6 Awarding bodies are notified of any changes to the personnel of the assessment and verification team.
2.2.7 Unit certification is made available to candidates.

3 MONITORING AND REVIEW

RECORDS

Criteria

3.1.1 Records of candidate details and achievements are complete, securely stored in line with awarding body requirements, and available for external verification and auditing.

3.1.2 Records of internal verification activity are maintained, up to date, and made available for the purposes of auditing.

3.1.3 Information supplied to the awarding body for the purposes of registration and certification is complete and accurate.

3.1.4 Information and recording systems enable candidates' achievements to be monitored and reviewed in relation to the centre's equal opportunities policy and action plan.

REVIEW

Criteria

3.2.1 Actions identified by external verification visits are disseminated to appropriate staff and corrective measures are implemented.

3.2.2 The effectiveness of the internal verification strategy is reviewed against national requirements and corrective measures are implemented.

3.2.3 Candidate, employer and other feedback is used to evaluate the quality and effectiveness of qualification provision against the centre's stated aims and policies, leading to continuous improvement.

3.2.4 The centre's achievements against its plan are monitored and reviewed and used to inform future centre qualification development activity.

APPENDIX D: SUMMARY OF THE ISO 9000 STANDARD

ISO 9001 requirement	Clause	Organization should specify
Management responsibility	4.1	
Quality policy	4.1.1	The quality policy
Organization	4.1.2	
Responsibility and authority	4.1.2.1	Which people's work affects product quality
Resources and trained personnel	4.1.2.2	What resources are needed
Management representative (quality system responsibility)	4.1.2.3	Who is the manager responsible for the quality system, who will implement, maintain and report on the system to senior management?
Management review	4.1.3	
Quality system	4.2	
General	4.2.1	The system's manual
Quality system procedures	4.2.2	The work instructions
Quality planning	4.2.3	How it will meet its quality needs
Contract review	4.3	
General	4.3.1	The systems for checking orders or contracts before they are fulfilled
Review	4.3.2	How each order will be checked to ensure it can be fulfilled
Amendment to contract	4.3.3	How changes are made to orders
Records	4.3.4	How the checking of orders is documented
Design control (Not part of ISO 9002)	4.4	
General	4.4.1	How the product is designed
Design and development planning/tests	4.4.2	The procedure for the planning of each design activity is planned and allocated

ISO 9001 requirement	Clause	Organization should specify
Organizational and technical interfaces	4.4.3	How people from different departments or sections communicate and interact
Design input	4.4.4	The information needed to create a design, how this is reviewed and implemented
Design output	4.4.5	The nature of progress meetings with all relevant people
Design review	4.4.6	How the designs are shown to meet the brief
Design verification	4.4.7	How designs are tested, checked and documented to have met the brief
Design validation	4.4.8	How the design is checked to ensure it meets the customer's needs
Design changes	4.4.9	The system for authorizing and making changes to a design
Document, data and specification control	4.5	
General	4.5.1	The system for controlling all quality related documents
Document and data approval and issue	4.5.2	The procedure for authorizing, verifying and issuing documents
Document and data changes and modifications	4.5.3	The system for making changes to quality related documents
Purchasing (control of purchases)	4.6	
General/responsibility	4.6.1	The system for ensuring purchases are fit for their intended purpose
Evaluation of sub-contractors (Supplier assessment)	4.6.2	The system for choosing suppliers and recording acceptable suppliers
Purchasing data	4.6.3	The system for producing, checking and approving purchase orders
Verification of purchased product	4.6.4	
Supplier verification at sub-contractor's premises	4.6.4.1	The system for checking your purchases at the supplier's premises

ISO 9001 requirement	Clause	Organization should specify
Customer verification of sub-contracted product	4.6.4.2	When do you wish your customer to check your purchases?
Control of customer supplied product	4.7	How you look after products which belong to your customer
Product identification and traceability	4.8	How you identify your product during and after its production
Process control	4.9	The system for monitoring and controlling the production process
Inspection and tests	4.10	
General	4.10.1	The system for inspecting and checking the quality of the process and product
Receiving inspection and testing	4.10.2	How you check goods and raw materials at goods inwards
In-process inspection and testing	4.10.3	How you check the quality of the product during the stages of production
Final inspection and testing	4.10.4	How you check the quality of the product at the end of the production process
Inspection and test records	4.10.5	How you record and document these checks
Inspection, measuring and test equipment	4.11	
General	4.11.1	The system for checking the accuracy of inspection equipment
Control procedure	4.11.2	The procedure for the checking and maintenance of inspection equipment
Inspection and test status (indication of)	4.12	The system for identifying whether or not, products have passed their inspection
Control of nonconforming product	4.13	
General	4.13.1	The system for the identification, recording and disposal of faulty products
Nonconformity review and disposition	4.13.2	The system for dealing with faulty products

ISO 9001 requirement	Clause	Organization should specify
Corrective action	4.14	
General	4.14.1	The system for implementing effective action to prevent faulty products
Corrective action	4.14.2	How you instigate corrective action to eliminate the production of faulty products
Recurring defect prevention	4.14.3	How you prevent faulty products being produced
Handling storage, packaging and delivery	4.15	
General	4.15.1	The system for the handling, storing, packing, preservation and delivery of products
Handling	4.15.2	How you handle your products
Storage	4.15.3	How you store your products
Packaging	4.15.4	How you package your products
Preservation	4.15.5	How you preserve your products
Delivery	4.15.6	How you deliver your products
Quality records	4.16	The system for recording, collecting and storing quality records
Internal quality audits	4.17	The system for auditing the quality system
Training	4.18	The system for identifying and meeting the learning needs of staff
Servicing	4.19	The system for servicing the product
SPC and statistical techniques	4.20	
Identification of need	4.20.1	How you assess the need for statistics to control quality
Procedures	4.20.2	How you collect and use statistics

APPENDIX E: CONTACT LIST

The Qualification and Curriculum Authority
222 Euston Road
London NW1 2BZ
Tel: 0171 387 9898
Fax: 0171 387 0978
e-mail: mail@qca.org.uk

The Scottish Qualification Authority
Hanover House
24 Douglas Street
Glasgow G2 7NQ
Tel: 0141 248 7900
Fax: 0141 242 2244
e-mail: mail@sqa.org.uk

Investors in People UK
4th Floor
7–10 Chandos Street
London W1M 9DE
Tel: 0171 467 1900
Fax: 0171 636 2386

REFERENCES

Argyris, C (1997) 'Double loop learning in organizations', in *Harvard Business Review*, **55**, 5, 115–25.

Argyris, C and Schön, D (1978) *Organisational Learning*, Addison-Wesley, Reading, Mass.

Barra, R (1989) *Putting Quality Circles to Work*, McGraw-Hill, New York.

Dorrell, J (1993) *Resource-based learning*, McGraw-Hill, New York.

Fletcher, C (1993) *Appraisal: Routes to Improved Performance*, Institute of Personnel Management, London.

Malhotra, Y (1996) *Organisational Learning and Learning Organisations: An Overview*, URL: http://www.brint.com/papers/orglrng.htm

Mansfield, B and Mathews, D (1985) in Jessup, G (1991) *Outcomes: NVQs and the Emerging Model of Education and Training*, Falmer Press, London.

Poell, R, Tijmensen, L and van der Krogt, F (1997) 'Can learning projects help to develop a learning organisation?', Lifelong Learning in Europe, **2**, 67–75.

Sadgrove, K (1994) *ISO9000/BS5750 Made Easy*, Kogan Page, London.

Swieringa, J and Wierdsma, A (1992) *Becoming a Learning Organization*, Addison-Wesley, Reading, Mass.

FURTHER READING

Argyris, C (1976) *Intervention Theory and Method: A Behavioural Science View*, Addison-Wesley, Reading, Mass.

Argyris, C (1994) *On Organisational Learning*, Blackwell Publishers Ltd, Oxford.

Bamber, AL (1992) *Look Up and Learn*, Library Association, London.

Billsberry, J (1996) *Finding and Keeping the Right People: How to Recruit Motivated Employees*, Pitman, London.

Bird, M (1992) *Effective Leadership*, BBC Books, London.

Buckley, R and Caple, J (1996) *One-to-One Training and Coaching Skills*, Kogan Page, London.

Burgoyne, J, Pedler, M and Boydell, T (1994) *Towards The Learning Company: Concepts and Practices*, McGraw-Hill, New York.

Dixon, NM 'Organisational learning: a review of the literature with implications for HRD professionals', *Human Resource Development Quarterly*, **3**, 1, 29–49.

Fletcher, S (1992) *Competence-based Assessment Techniques*, Kogan Page, London.

Flood, RL (1995) *Solving Problem Solving*, John Wiley & Sons Ltd, Chichester.

Francis, D (1987) *Organisational Communication*, Wildwood House Ltd, Aldershot.

Hill, WF (1990) *Learning: A Survey of Psychological Interpretations*, 5th edn, Harper & Row, New York.

Jessup, G (1991) *Outcomes: NVQs and the Emerging Model of Education and Training*, The Falmer Press, London.

Maddux, RB (1988) *Effective Performance Appraisals*, Kogan Page, London.

Mulrooney, C and Pearn, M (1997) 'The chicken and the egg: lifelong learning and the learning organisation', in *Lifelong Learning in Europe*, **2**, 76–81.

NCVQ (1997) *The Awarding Bodies' Common Accord*, NCVQ, London.

Parsloe, E (1992) *Coaching Mentoring and Assessing*, Kogan Page, London.

Revans, R (1983) *The ABC of Action Learning*, Chartwell-Bratt.

Rickards, T (1974) *Problem Solving Through Creative Analysis*, Gower, Aldershot.

Robson, M (1988) *Quality Circles: A Practical Guide*, Gower, Aldershot.

Rowntree, D (1990) *Teaching Through Self-instruction: How to Develop Open Learning Materials*, Kogan Page, London.

Wilson, DC (1992) *A Strategy of Change*, Routledge, London.

INDEX